MARKINGS
my own

Published in association with Eastern Mennonite University.

MARKINGS *my own*

Musings on the Gospel of Mark

Omar Eby

Foreword by Lee Snyder

DreamSeeker Books
TELFORD, PENNSYLVANIA

an imprint of
Cascadia Publishing House

Copublished with
Herald Press
Scottdale, Pennsylvania

Cascadia Publishing House orders, information, reprint permissions:
contact@CascadiaPublishingHouse.com
1-215-723-9125
126 Klingerman Road, Telford PA 18969
www.CascadiaPublishingHouse.com

Markings/My Own
DreamSeeker Books is an imprint of
Cascadia Publishing House
Copublished with Herald Press, Scottdale, PA
Library of Congress Catalog Number: 2003048874
ISBN: 1-931038-18-X
Printed in Canada by Pandora Press
Book design by Cascadia Publishing House
Cover design by Gwen M. Stamm

Grateful acknowledgment is made for materials used by permission, all rights reserved:
Thomas H. Troeger excerpts pp. 27-28 from *Borrowed Light* © 1994 Oxford University Press, Inc.; Thomas Merton excerpts pp. 66-67 from *The Wisdom of the Desert*, copyright © 1960 by the Abbey of Gethsemani, Inc. Reprinted by permission of New Directions Publishing Corp.; Ernest Becker excerpts pp. 174-175 reprinted with the permission of The Free Press, A Division of Simon & Schuster Adult Publishing Group, from *The Denial of Death*, by Ernest Becker. Copyright © 1973 by the Free Press. Unless otherwise noted, Bible quotations are the author's paraphrase but based on *The Holy Bible, New International Version,* copyright 1973, 1978, 1984 International Bible Society, Zondervan Bible Publishers, and sometimes modified by *The King James Version of The Bible* (KJV).

Library of Congress Cataloguing-in-Publication Data

Eby, Omar, 1935-
    Markings / my own: musings on the Gospel of Mark / Omar Eby.
      p. cm.
    Includes bibliographical references.
    ISBN 1-931038-18-X (alk. paper)
     1. Bible. N.T. Mark--Commentaries. I. Title

BS2585.53.E29 2003
226.3'06--dc21

                   2003048874
10 09 08 07 06 05 04 03   10 9 8 7 6 5 4 3 2 1

Contents

Foreword

"DON'T MISS THE TABLE OF CONTENTS," is the first instruction in picking up *Markings/My Own.* It is a tantalizing outline, daring the reader to enter into musings on the Gospel of Mark: "Fish and chips," "No pigs in the peaceable kingdom?" or "Grain and Whine." This is vintage Omar Eby, signaling what is in store for those who are ready to be prodded, startled, even outraged, and finally blessed by these insightful meditations on how the Son of God reveals himself to his disciples.

"'We must plunge into experience and then reflect on the meaning of it,'" says Eby, quoting from a favorite author. In this work, the reader is swept into both the New Testament experiences of Jesus and his followers and into the world of a witty, gritty writer who intertwines personal memoir with reflections on the biblical story. These meditations are refracted through the hopes, desires, and struggles of one man very much in touch with his humanity. With ruthless honesty and teasing provocation, the writer reveals a deep reverence for God's mysterious way with his creatures.

This is a story of inherited faith but also an account of a hard-won faith. Heightening a sense of the search for the divine in the ordinary is the particularity of place. From Capernaum to Jerusalem, from Paris to Mogadishu, from the Shenandoah Valley to the Serengeti Plains, from a retired professor's back garden to the African savannas, the traveler on the journey of faith is irresistibly pulled along. These meditations on the Scripture signal an immersion into experience itself, which God honors through this writer/poet's renderings of the sights, sounds, yearnings, delights, and fears of everyday life.

Of particular interest to those who draw sustenance from the creative work of artists, writers, and musicians are the references to artists who help us mourn and celebrate life, who give us insights into the deeper meaning of our existence, and who thus urge us to noble callings and faithful commitments. These "markings" are a literature lover's feast. I found myself watching for the references to the greats: Gerard Manley Hopkins, William Blake, John Milton, Edmund Spenser, William Shakespeare, John Bunyan, John Donne, Ben Jonson, George Herbert, Andrew Marvell, Alexander Pope, Francis Bacon, William Wordsworth, Robert Browning, Samuel Coleridge, John Ruskin, Thomas Carlyle, Ben Franklin, Francis Thompson, John Keats, W. B. Yeats, Algernon Charles Swinburne, Goethe, Thomas Mann, T. S. Eliot, James Joyce and Virginia Woolf, W. H. Auden, Dylan Thomas, Thomas Mann, Fyodor Dostoevsky, Leo Tolstoy, Henrik Ibsen, Ralph Waldo Emerson, Henry David Thoreau, Nathaniel Hawthorne, Herman Melville.

It becomes a game—the hunt for these rich literary citations. But there are more: Joseph Conrad, C. S. Lewis, E. M. Forster, John Updike, Samuel Beckett, William Faulkner, Ernest Hemingway, John Ciardi, Ezra Pound, Robert Frost, Kahlil Gibran, Graham Greene, Reynolds Price, Harper Lee, Thornton Wilder, James Baldwin, J. B. Priestley, James Weldon Jones, Annie Dillard, Frederick Buechner, Mitch Albom, and Kathleen Norris.

We understand the gospel story better when we catch glimpses of what Jesus becoming one of us means in our setting. Here Mark's Gospel, with a cast of wonderfully human characters, is writ large through the perspective and personas of Omar Eby—author, Anabaptist, colleague, descendant, friend, horticulturist, grandparent, gourmand, teacher, mentor, missionary, music lover, parent, pilgrim, poet, seeker, sinner, and spouse.

This book is for reflectives who find their souls nurtured by the music of Mozart, Bach, Handel, Randall Thompson, or Andrew Lloyd Webber. The references to Michelangelo, Monet, Van Gogh, Constable, Bruegel, Hieronymus Bosch, or Salvador Dali become for the reader a persuasive example of how the creative spirits and artists among us nourish the soul and accompany us on the journey of faith. Rounding out these strands of literature, art and music are the frequent acknowledgements of those spiritual seekers who continue to inspire or challenge the pilgrim's search for God: Nietzsche, Bonhoeffer, Freud, Ernest Becker, Teilhard de Chardin, Kierkegaard, Henri Nouwen, Thomas Merton, Charles Sheldon, John Howard Yoder.

These lists are more than samplings of sources, both past and present, from which Omar Eby draws to examine a life—his life. These individuals, as well as nature, become companions along the way. "The physical world embodies a spiritual world, concealed from those who have eyes only for the glitter of Broadway or the glitz of tele-evangelists," Omar Eby observes. "Saints discover that all living and growing manifestations of nature give glory to God by being exactly what he has destined them to be."

This book will appeal to a wide range of readers—to lovers of Scripture, to seekers of understanding, to the person who responds to a clever turn of phrase or appreciates the discomfort of introspection. *Markings* does not offer pious niceties. With a bent toward survival by wit and a love of the outrageous, the author conveys, paradoxically perhaps, a gracious witness to the incomparable ways of God among humankind.

A keen observer of nature and human nature—acquainted with the ache of the human spirit, its beauty, sorrow, disappointment and hope—Omar Eby shares the consolations of remembering and imagining. Fellow pilgrims seeking comfort and renewal will not be disappointed in joining the author in search of life-giving Word. This is a book of witness and worship and I commend it to all those fellow travelers on the journey of faith.

—*Lee Snyder, President*
Bluffton (Oh.) College

Author's Preface: Toward an Apology and a Dedication

I WAS A FLOUNDERING ENGLISH TEACHER IN A BOYS' secondary school at Musoma, Tanzania, 1966-1967. To restore fractured psychic poise, I often sat out under the flowering mimosa tree on weekends, my back to a school as regimented as a boot camp. There in leaf-flecked shade I gazed out over wide, quiet Lake Victoria, and read the Gospel of Mark and Dag Hammarskjold's *Markings*.

I brought with me to East Africa his posthumously published reflections as a mute Christian while in the United Nation's courts of intrigue and diplomacy. In addition to English classes, my Aussie headmaster assigned me to teach Bible Knowledge, that year the Gospel of Mark. I was to prepare thirty-five Form IV boys for their Cambridge Overseas School Certificate "O" Level Examinations. Thus, over the past thirty-five years Mark and *Markings* are often joined when I recall that African classroom.

The arrival of Mark did not surprise me when I sat down to work that first morning of my early retirement. No excuses now for failing to practice anew some of the old spiritual disciplines: Bible study, meditation, prayer, contemplation, silence. (I deliberately excluded fasting. I did not eat lunches for twenty-seven years while at the college. Now I would give thanks for the noon apple—obligatory and ubiquitous!) A more severe discipline for me is writing. Well, then, let me suffer. So, I added writing to my practice of these austere disciplines. To void spiritual narcissism, I focused, not on a withered heart, but on holy Scripture. Thus, Mark arrived, under whom I would make my own *Markings*.

I studied each episode in Mark's Gospel (sixty-two, altogether), morning-by-morning-by-morning. And I let the past forty years of my life—teaching literature at the college level, reading and writing, listening to music, walking in the orchard and woods, living in Africa, heeding one wise woman, rearing children, stumbling toward God—play against the Markian episode. Then, under the influence of that episode I would write—four hours only, three pages only.

My musings are not commentary nor traditional meditations. Rather, they blend intellectual inquiry with confessional worship, meld poignancy, whimsy, grit, doubt, sorrow, and inspiration. A spiritual memoir. Since the topics change constantly, the style is deliberately eclectic, organic to the Markian text.

Here now are my own markings, personal musings on the spare but elegant Gospel of Mark. I hope it can be said of my writing, as did one British critic of C. S. Lewis: "He makes righteousness readable."

I write first to exercise my own soul. Then for my children—Katrina and Michael, Maria and Brent, Lawrence and Melanie—to aid them in owning an inherited faith. I write also for those former university students who keep in touch, who share with me their own "awful rowings toward God"—or, sorrowfully, away.

If there are any thanks for what is written here, then let it be "*Ad Majorem Dei Gloriam*."

—Omar Eby
Harrisonburg, Virginia, 2003

Acknowledgments

FOUR OLD FRIENDS AND COLLEAGUES LAID aside congeniality and sat down to this manuscript with editorial pens as sharp as scalpels: James R. Bomberger, Hubert R. Pellman, Millie Pellman, and Carroll Yoder. I thank them for their severe mercy.

To Michael A. King, chief editor and publisher: thanks for his generous care of this writer. Anna Kathryn (Shenk) Eby, my wife, needs special gratitude. She allowed me to retire early from the university classroom and seek no other employment but to sit down and write. Still she went out the door every morning, happily, to her third-grade classroom. And gave me a generous monthly allowance from her salary, and never asked how I spent it. Special thanks to Elmer J. and Martha Ann Miller for their financial support.

Also, I am grateful for the support from Eastern Mennonite University, Harrisonburg, Virginia.

MARKINGS

my own

The Wilderness and the River
John the Baptist Prepares the Way

So John appeared in the wilderness, preaching a baptism of repentance, baptizing in the Jordan River. —Mark 1:1-8

JOHN WAS NOT THE FIRST to respond to the impulse that draws seekers into the wilderness. The discovery of the Dead Sea Scrolls reveals a Jewish monastic community established in the hardscrabble wilderness. East of fashionable Jerusalem, the center of Jewish religion and culture, and on the western shores of the Dead Sea, the sect found solace in fierce landscape. Possibly John himself associated with them. Luke declares in his gospel: "John lived out in the wilderness until the day he appeared publicly to Israel" (1:80).

The youthful Moses, having slain an Egyptian, fled to the wilderness. Then, as a middle-aged statesman, he wandered forty years in the wilderness with a disgruntled people. King David fled his throne from a mutinous son to the wilderness. Jesus withdrew for forty days into the wilderness. In the fourth and fifth centuries of the Christian era a few wise, worried men and women walked into the deserts of Egypt, Palestine, Arabia, and Persia, and turned their backs on a Christian emperor who made

of Christ's cross a sign of temporal power. On a quest for salvation, these first Christian hermits lived in the wilderness for the
rest of their lives. Today, many Christians retreat from frenetic
urban life to a cabin, to a farm, to a desert. There in the wilderness, God touches some.

I have often felt the lure of the wilderness: known the or-
chards and woodlots of my boyhood, walked in the silver-gray
Somali thorn bush, driven slowly over the long tawny flanks of
the Serengeti Plains during my young adult years. For two
decades now I've felt the draw of the Blue Ridge Mountains and
far empty meadows of the Shenandoah Valley. Chiefly such envi-
ronments provide silence and solitude.

A saint attentive to nature hears in the mountains, the
deserts, the savannas another language of God, not just the Hebrew and Aramaic tongue of the Testaments. The physical world
embodies a spiritual world, concealed from those who have eyes
only for the glitter of Broadway or the glitz of tele-evangelists.
Saints discover that all living and growing manifestations of nature give glory to God by being exactly what he has destined
them to be. This is something of the "inscape" of which poet
Gerard Manley Hopkins writes, this inarticulate utterance by a
natural object of an identity which it has from and in God; this
inexhaustible spiritual sheen radiates out through the fragile film
of matter.

If the ocean praises God with its majestic restlessness, so
does this sun-blanched savanna praise God with its horizons, its
grasses afire in the scintillating heat. So, too the heat-blistered
red rock canyons, the strewn stone rivers without water. Even the
high heavens, brassy-white with a stalled sun, clapper out great
round gongs of glory.

I often read the geography of the Old Testament saga, the
landscape of Jesus' ministry: the wilderness—the deserts and
mountains—and river settings, the many stories set elsewhere in
Jordan Valley villages. I read the lives and writings of the fifth
century desert saints, filtered through the contemporary
Thomas Mertons. One recent summer an additionally engross-

ing read was Belden C. Lane's *The Solace of Fierce Landscapes: Exploring Desert and Mountain Spirituality.* Part memoir, part commentary, part historical review—all parts a fitting blend to make the whole reading of the book cause for reflection and thanks for sustenance from an ancient spiritual tradition.

What we learn in the wilderness, Lane tells us, is often a harsh truth: God is more given to silence than speech. Our endlessly anxious ego, given to self-realization, must empty itself out before God can enter. God's fiery love moves us toward an ascetic life, *la via negativa.* Even the old Christian still leans toward, though he may never know fully, that dangerous ache of self-obliteration. He finds in Thomas Merton's description of an old desert father the pattern of his own quest. "He could not retain the slightest identification with his superficial, transient, self-constructed self. He had to lose himself in the inner, hidden reality of a self that was transcendent, mysterious, half-known, and lost in Christ" (*The Wisdom of the Desert*, 7).

Silence, solitude. prayer. In the wilderness, John's spirit is refined, his life simplified. He transcends the nonessentials. He comes girdled in a loin cloth of camel hair, eating roasted locust dipped in wild honey. The stylish, fickle urbanites walk a day into the bush, endure a scouring message, enter the muddy Jordan for a baptism. They imagine themselves as transformed as the rough Baptizer, who came out of solitude and silence with a message of repentance, a prophecy about One he hardly knows of whom he speaks: a vision from the wilderness. He risks to act on his intensely personal experience of a fresh health borne by the call of wild terrain.

Sometimes even our worst selves yearn for a season of silence and solitude in the wilderness, for another baptism of sorrow—a public declaration in our mid-adult years to dedicate one's energies toward a more simple life, even an ascetic life. How, then, to nurture that call.

The River and the Ditch
The Baptism and Temptation of Jesus

Jesus was baptized in the Jordan. . . . A voice from heaven said: "Thou Art my son, my Beloved." . . . Immediately the Spirit drove him into the wilderness. —Mark 1:9-13

WHERE IN THE JORDAN RIVER did John baptize Jesus? His parental home was in Nazareth, a town not mentioned in the Old Testament. In the New Testament, when told by Philip that he had found "Jesus of Nazareth," Nathaniel sneers, "Can anything good come from there?" Did that watery ceremony take place a dozen miles east of his boyhood town, at the fords of the Jordan to the Decapolis? Or had Jesus walked four days, eighty miles south to Jerusalem and then east to the Jordan at Qumran, the Baptist's Essene community? There at the mouth of the Jordan where it flows into the Dead Sea?

Jesus stood somewhere in the Jordan, an Arabic word for "the downrusher." Well-named or nicknamed, because between its source near Caesarea Philippi to where it enters the Dead Sea, the Jordan drops from 1,200 feet above sea level to 1,200 feet below, meandering 200 miles to cover a distance of sixty-five miles, as the crow flies. The Jordan Valley is a part of that vast fault running from the Beka'a Valley in the Lebanons down through Palestine to the Gulf of Aqabah, to the Red Sea, to the Great Rift Valley of East Africa, to Lakes Victoria, Tanganyika, and Malawi.

So Jesus stood in that deepest ditch in the world's crust. He stood in the gap—a wonderfully fitting symbolic act: Jesus steps into that fissure between his divine Father and his human brothers and sisters, a first gesture of learning about becoming a suffering servant, about his life ministry, about his "father's business"—terrible yet necessary. Of which, later, St. Paul would write to the Corinthian Greeks, "All is from God, who reconciled us to himself through Christ, . . . indeed God has reconciled the whole world to himself through Christ. . ." (2 Cor. 5:18, 19). Jesus, then, is both the God-man standing in a watery gulch and "a bridge over troubled waters."

So Jesus stood in that gap and saw the heavens "torn" open, saw the Spirit descend on him "like a dove," heard a voice clap, if not in the lush thickets on the river's banks, at least inside his skull: "You are my Beloved Son." Such urgency in the word *torn*; such tenderness in the metaphor *dove*. Such juxtaposition of opposites is underscored by the next act.

Henri Nouwen, writing in *Life of the Beloved*, declares that a person today can hear that same Voice announcing belovedness even as the divine son once did. Nouwen offers an interpretation of that phrase, "You are my Beloved"—what he heard for himself: "I have called you by name, from the very beginning. You are mine and I am yours. You are my Beloved, on you my favor rests. I have molded you in the depths of the earth and knitted you together in your mother's womb. I have carved you on the palms of my hands and hidden you in the shadow of my embrace. I look at you with infinite tenderness and care for you with a care more intimate than that of a mother for her child. I have counted every hair on your head and guided you at every step. Wherever you go, I go with you, and wherever you rest, I keep watch. I will give you food that will satisfy all your hunger and drink that will quench all your thirst. I will not hide my face from you. You know me as your own as I know you as my own.

You belong to me. I am your father, your mother, your brother, your sister, your lover, your spouse. . . . Nothing will ever separate us. We are one" (30, 31).

No sooner had the Spirit anointed Jesus as Son than the Spirit "drove" him into the wilderness. From the river to the wilderness, reversing his cousin John's pilgrimage. Again, an action verb of urgency: *drove*. Lest Jesus imagine Sonship accorded him pampering and divine indulgence, he is thrown not only to the hyenas and jackals of the bush but to the Evil One: to Satan, whose Hebrew name means "the Opposition"; to the Devil, whose Greek name means "the Liar." Immediately Jesus faces the severe test: am I indeed the Beloved Son? Why not use my awful power for self-realization?

All Christians must go from the euphoric state of feeling the blessed child of God to the neglected child—abandoned in a wilderness not entirely of our own making. And for some that test period lasts not just forty days and nights—but forty years of terror and loneliness, with wild animals, scavengers of the spirit, lying in wait.

Then one day, it is all over! Angels minister to the bruised and hungry soul. And the Christian learns that while grace comes through some strange angels more often it comes through the common and domesticated ones: through a spouse, a neighbor, an unlikely friend, a student, even one's own child, the Eucharist, and nature—and even the ditch and the wilderness.

3

....

Fishing and Following
The Calling of the
First Disciples

Walking by the shore of the Sea of Galilee, Jesus saw Simon and his brother Andrew on the lake. "Come, follow me." They left their nets. . . . A little further Jesus saw James and his brother John. He called them; they left their father in the boat with the hired men. —Mark 1:14-20

WITH JOHN THE BAPTIST IMPRISONED in Jerusalem, Jesus travels home to Galilee, that northernmost province of Palestine, a land of fertile soil and a fertile cultural mix. The tribes of Asher, Naphtali, and Zebulum never succeeded in dispossessing the original Canaanite residents of their land and villages. Later, a series of Syrian, Aramaean, and Assyrian wars left behind a detritus of peoples. Later Greeks too. And by Jesus' time, the Romans a final overlay.

Fertile and well-watered Galilean plains lay between the Galilean Sea to the east and the mountain range to the west. Rich pastureland for flocks and grain, a climate for olives and dates. There today oranges and apples grow within a few miles elevation from each other. From the Sea of Galilee, lying nearly 700 feet below sea level, fish—fresh, dried, pickled—were shipped over the old camel caravan routes and later Roman stone-paved roads, some even as far as Spain. Thus Jesus' Jewish Galilean people were in daily contact with Greek and Roman cultures. Less

orthodox than their Jerusalem pure-blue-blooded Jewish brothers and sisters, Galileans were looked down on as people who had
not earned the right to be taken seriously in discussions about interpretations of the Law.

From Galilean people Jesus calls eleven of his twelve disciples. Only Judas, the sole Judean, is from the south. That first
day's calling yields two pairs of fishermen brothers: Simon and
Andrew, James and John. One might read this as tribal, clannish,
parochial. Better understood is that the Galilean with broader
exposure to cultures other than orthodox Jewry will more
quickly catch the vision of Jesus' New Community.

"Come, follow me." I cannot write this phrase and not think
of Bonhoeffer. From prison he writes, "When Jesus calls a man,
he bids him come and die." One remembers too the poetic language of Gerard Manley Hopkins, in sonnets of exaltation and
sonnets of desolation: "crushed," "buckle," "pitched." Merci-
fully, only a few saints, such as Hopkins, following the Son are
crushed by the experience. As though that oil or juice—an
essence—is a greater manifestation of God's grandeur than are
the ripe fruits. One finds this truth in lines from each of Hopkins' six Dublin sonnets of desolation. To follow Christ is not always to know easily the comfort of affirmation.

> O thou terrible, why wouldst thou rude on me
> Thy wring-world right foot rock? lay a lionlimb against me?
> Scan with darksome devouring eyes my bruised bones?
>
> Comforter, where, where is your comforting?
> I am gall, I am heartburn. God's most deep decree
> Bitter would have me taste: my taste was me;
>
> Wert thou my enemy, O thou my friend,
> How wouldst thou worse, I wonder. . . .
> birds build—but not I build; no, but strain,
> Time's eunuch, and not breed one work that wakes.
> Mine, O thou lord of life, send my roots rain.

To affirm the harsh experiences of our lives—so contrary to our modern psycho-theology, which pampers the ego's province of self-realization, rather than submitting to self-abnegation.

I think too of those whom Jesus did not call: Father Zebedee and his hired men who still went on fishing, after the sons set out to follow a minor provincial rabbi. My heart is with them, has known their surprise at an imagined divine neglect. To establish his school, Jesus didn't need all to follow him. In fact, one man cleansed of devils (which slaughtered a herd of pigs!) begged to go with Jesus, but he strictly forbade it: "Go home to your own folks and tell them..." (5:18-19).

So when Africa closed to me twice, I was to learn that I could not abandon my college teaching vocation but must learn "to follow"—to come and die to the self that wanted to serve Christ in a manner I thought best. Emptied out again and again into the reading of 10,000 freshmen comps, I learned to follow in ordinary work, quite ordinary work. Work and not whine—well, only a little!

For me there was to be no traipsing around Africa with Jesus and his elite disciples. It was back to salting down and preserving first-year college writers, from whom might come one with a special calling to be taken in for private training among Christ's personal disciples to experience a privileged, even an elitist, camaraderie. And from my severe affectionate attention to their writing would come more than one who would go on to write better fiction and philosophical reflections than I.

An Evil Spirit in a Stone Synagogue
Jesus Drives out an Unclean Spirit

They went to Capernaum, and on the Sabbath Jesus went into the synagogue and began to teach. . . . A man possessed by an evil spirit cried out, "I know you—the Holy One of God!" —Mark 1:21-28

ABOUT CAPERNAUM, A SMALL TOWN on the Sea of Galilee, the town fathers could boast of its fishing harbor, the regional tax office, the Roman military garrison, and a handsome 200-year-old synagogue of white limestone.

It's to this synagogue that Jesus takes his first clutch of disciples that first sabbath after their calling, to launch his public ministry. Capernaum, not Nazareth, his hometown, where earlier he had preached to the Nazarites (Luke 4:14-30). On that one occasion the home town boy so infuriated his neighbors that they threatened to murder him. After that debacle Jesus never again returned to try to teach his home folks. Rather, he launched his Galilean ministry from Capernaum.

If Jesus had at least nine of his twelve disciples, he handily brought with him the obligatory quorum of ten adult males to conduct a synagogue service. Not all the pious Jewish mothers of

Capernaum and nine males could publicly invoke the divine presence. This was an assembly of men; yet, women could observe or participate from their own gallery. With this custom, Jesus seems little perturbed. More likely, he probably had only two sets of fishermen brothers with him that day.

Maybe the Galileans, tough fishermen, did not attend this synagogue in Capernaum; finding its elegance uncomfortable, they worshiped in another lake town. Archeological digs have unearthed a fine piece of religious architecture. Luke suggests the Capernaum synagogue was built by the local centurion, a Roman ruler of whom the Jewish townspeople declared, "He loves our nation and has built our synagogue!" (7:5).

Maybe that accounts for its handsome stone columns, its white lime flagstone floors covered with woven rush mats, its carved stone benches. But of particular interest to our eye are the stone carvings on the frieze: not just geometrical figures, but palm trees, stars, lions and eagles! Whatever happened to "Thou shalt not make unto thee any graven images"?

Little Capernaum has a quaint cosmopolitan air in which Jesus is comfortable. In just such a sea resort with its tropical climate and slight urban air, Jesus sits and talks of an upside-down kingdom. He expounds the old law with new authority. Not of the Scribes, those doctors of religious and moral jurisprudence, this itinerant teacher further demonstrates authority with an instant cure by exorcism. An evil, unclean spirit proclaims a truth: "You (Jesus) are the Holy one of God!"

But Jesus clamps him shut! Perhaps in the manner of Thomas H. Troeger's words,

"Silence! frenzied, unclean spirit,"
Cried God's healing, holy One.
"Cease your ranting! Flesh can't bear it.
Flee as night before the sun."
At Christ's voice the demon trembled,
From its victim madly rushed,
While the crowd that was assembled
Stood in wonder, stunned and hushed.

How I'd love to sing those words, snarl them out into the pious-loaded sanctuary! But the congregation never sings that hymn, not even the choir. I enjoy them during the too-long period of announcements.

One can imagine this evil spirit in the synagogue recognized the Jesus it had first met in the wilderness. His evil presence now here in the town's synagogue is a foreshadowing: even in the sacred place sits the Spirit of Opposition, the Devil of the Wilderness. This, the first of many occasions on which the Evil Spirit of Opposition to Good is uncovered in the holy places of Palestinian homes, lake sides, cornfields, temple, and cemetery. In a place of white limestone elegance, the resident demon was rebuked, then, and now is silenced in our current institutional correlatives of business, worship, government, and home.

Evil must be renounced, even though it attempts a disguise by uttering a truth. Such an utterance of truth is self-serving, an attempt at self-preservation. In the fine white sanctuary of our hearts too the self-preserving whispers of the insatiably hungry ego must be silenced, exorcised by a rebuke from our Lord.

Again, in the words of Troeger's 1984 hymn,

Lord, the demons still are thriving
In the grey cells of the mind:
Tyrant voices, shrill and driving,
Twisted thoughts that grip and bind,
Doubts that stir the heart to panic,
Fears distorting reason's sight,
Guilt that makes our loving frantic,
Dreams that cloud the soul with fright.
Silence, Lord, the unclean spirit,
In our mind and in our heart.
Speak your word that when we hear it
All our demons shall depart.
Clear our thought and calm our feeling
Still the fractured, warring soul.
By the power of your healing
Make us faithful, true and whole.

....

Fish and Chips
Jesus Heals Many

*Simon's mother-in-law lay in bed with a fever. . . . Jesus helped her up
and she began to wait on them. . . . After sunset the whole town gathered at the door. . . . Jesus healed many but did not let the demons
speak because they knew Him —Mark 1:29-34*

AFTER A DAY OF PUBLIC DISCOURSE in the local synagogue, Jesus ac-
cepts an invitation for dinner in a private home. It would be
blustery, back-slapping, iron-muscled Simon, in full beard, because he was married—Simon Peter, *Petros*, the rock, hard-
headed, but soft-hearted. He invited all the guys from the office
home for supper. He looked forward to a quiet tete-a-tete over a
few beers with Jesus about that casting out of a shrieking demon.
But nothing was ever calm around this impetuous man. Generous of heart, he had earlier welcomed his wife's mother and his
own kid brother Andy to come live in his own household. Again
it was not to be a quiet evening.

Simon's house was in Bethsaida, a Hebrew word for "house
of fishermen," a fishing village suburb to Capernaum. In that
lake-side bungalow, Simon's mother-in-law lay with a fever, the
malaria season again full of mosquitoes. No mention is made of
Ms. Simon. Perhaps she died in childbirth; but more likely she
was pregnant again and indisposed. Whatever, no woman was
handy to broil bream in lemon butter and dill.

So Jesus performs his second cure of the day. He raises Simon's mother-in-law from her mat, clears her burning head. Dutifully, this nameless woman "waits on the men." How many? Well, at least five: her son-in-law and his brother, another set of brother fishermen, common drop-ins; the surprise visitor is the provincial itinerant evangelist, Jesus Somebody. With so many men's appetites to feed, perhaps Mom-in-law wished she could have remained feverish in bed. Was this your common man's view of a situation: cure the woman so she can wait on the men?

I think otherwise. Cured and grateful, she wanted to serve. Perhaps she had heard the town gossip; after all, "news about him spread quickly over the whole region" (1:28). She felt her kitchen honored by this man's visit. Earlier, when he knelt by her mat, touching her with healing in his hands, she'd shot a glance in panic at the cluttered bedroom. Messy, messy Simon would not hang up his night gown, would not keep his fishing gear out on the veranda. Now, to make amends for her son-in-law's happy slovenliness, she'd whip up a tasty batch of fish and chips.

But at 6:00 o'clock, sunset, the Sabbath ended, and all hell broke loose! Her little home swarmed with the town idlers and curiosity seekers. But worse: people sick with unpronounceable contagious diseases, even a few lepers and the village idiot, crowded the veranda. Indeed, she was later to say to Mark: "The whole town gathered at the door!" Hyperbolic but forgivable in a woman only recently cured and looking up from frying fish to find her darkened kitchen window filled with townspeople, some with whom she had but a mere nodding acquaintance, others, her old gossips at the town's communal water spigot.

Lordy! but the sight of this herd was enough to send her straight back to bed—yet then she remembered her distinguished guest, a man with healing in his hands. So she banged her iron skillet joyfully and whistled, "Saved to serve!"—knowing its truth more deeply in her heart than the tinny sound of its popular melody could release.

But Jesus did not heal "all the sick and demon-possessed." Mark records carefully: "Jesus healed *many*" (italics mine!). Not all who said, "Lord, Lord, did we not rush out here after worship to Simon's house to have an evil spirit cast out—?" And to all of those demons wrenched from Capernaum townspeople, Jesus spoke severely: "Shut up! I command you to be mute. Although you know me from our encounter in the wilderness, I forbid you to name me!" And rightly so. I think of this with my one-minute surfings of a religious television channel. Some Christian celebrities who've made themselves in the image of the Hollywood diva or an entrepreneurial Trump should not declare the simple Galilean's name together with their narcissistic babble. They stun the unbeliever.

The mother-in-law knew, too, the truth about her visitor. Like the demons now released in her house and rattling her crockery and utensils and whipping up her fire too high with their evil breath—she too said nothing. But she pondered these things in her heart. Perhaps she wouldn't even risk telling about this evening's holy events to her old gossips tomorrow morning at the village well.

This mother-in-law of Simon—who himself later became one of Jesus' three favorites, who still later as an apostle is always listed first—this nameless woman is like Mr. Zebedee and the hired men not called by Jesus. Unlike her son-in-law, she must stay in the kitchen and cook. Like that later saint, Brother Lawrence of seventeenth century France, this woman too could say, "The time of business does not with me differ from the time of prayer; and in the noise and clatter of my kitchen, while several persons are at the same time calling for different things, I possess God in as great tranquility as if I were upon my knees at the blessed sacrament."

Before Dawn
Jesus Prays in
a Solitary Place

Early in the dark morning, Jesus walked to a solitary place to pray. . . . When Simon and the brothers found him, they exclaimed: "Everyone is looking for you!" Jesus said, Let's go elsewhere to preach. . . . That's why I came. So they walked throughout Galilee. —Mark 1:35-38

HERE ARE THE INGREDIENTS OF A Romantic poem: a lake-side setting, a solitary character, a dawn—maybe even "a dapple-drawn-dawn." There flashes to mind lines from a sonnet by Wordsworth, that young father of British Romantic poetry:

> Earth has not anything to show more fair. . .
> The city now doth, like a garment, wear
> The beauty of the morning; . . .
> Ne'er saw I, never felt, a calm so deep!

The still lake mirrors the thin gauze of clouds, Monet in pastel color; the Golan Heights, a dark shoulder in silhouette. The rose-blush skies light up a rabbi walking, arms out, hands open, lips moving in prayer. But the character's intensity drains the scene of its romantic skein. Even God's Son prays!

His religious training held few if any instructions or restrictions concerning time, place, or posture for private prayers. Here, Jesus has slipped out of Simon's house before day-break.

One wonders who in that household gave up a bed for the visiting preacher. One hopes it wasn't that busy busy mother-in-law, who'd only just cleaned up after a late broken meal of fish and chips and wine, the men talking on and on about demon-possession and exorcism, and she, dead on her feet, still needing to stay up to wait on these men. Perhaps Jesus shared a mat with the horny young Andy; perhaps the teenage sons of Simon also lay about in this men's room. Jesus prayed. I like to think that quite possibly we hear in his later public "Lord's Prayer," phrases first formed here:

"My father who art in heaven!"—kinship keenly felt because of their far separation.

"Thy kingdom come"—a divine splendor and camaraderie and equity here break into this smug human economy.

"Daily bread"—on foot through provincial towns let someone be generous to a touring team of hungry men.

"Lead me not into temptation"—let the successful casting out of demons and the popularity of this one town not distract.

Like many other imitators of Christ, I too seek the solitary place—the meadow, the orchard, the woods behind our house. Sometimes the time and place are a gift. Wife off to her third-grade classroom, the house now emptied of lovely but distracting people, I am alone at the dining room table, rummaging the old heart before the fresh Word, writing down these thoughts chiefly for myself, distracted by only the brown thrasher; jittery, twitching, mute, it stalks the lawn, its song once described by Thoreau as a kissing sound!

I also walk narrow country roads at mid-afternoon before the fat school buses brush me aside into ditches filled with blue chicory and with Queen Anne's white lace on stalks. Those days when I'm feeling fragile, I walk the rubbery level track around the university men's soccer fields. I mean to make of each five-minute lap a time of prayer for individual people in my life: for a too-busy spouse, for the grown daughters and son and their spouses; for our granddaughters; for a dozen former students who keep in touch.

Often the prayers are little more than naming a person, over and over, my memories of experiences with that person, naming, too, that person's dreams. But too often I am distracted by the giant oaks in Park Woods, the crows in the open skies above the playing fields, the azure-hung Massanutten Peak. Like with Gerard Manley Hopkins, in "Hurrahing in the Harvest," I find that "I walk, I lift up, I lift up heart, eyes / Down all that glory in the heavens to glean our Saviour!" Hopkins makes of "down"—a preposition—a verb! I make of his sonnet a praise-prayer on my solitary walk around the track.

Such reverie is disturbed too soon by accusatory friends. "Everyone is looking for you!" Perhaps Simon's mother-in-law made a quiche with goat cheese, olives, and anchovies. Now it had all gone cold, and the chai had lost its fine Mediterranean bouquet. Perhaps more townspeople who had missed out on last night's healing service on Simon's veranda had brought their cripples. Even old Zebediah, ninety years on a gimpy leg, had hobbled across town and awaited a miracle.

Against all that appeal Jesus said to his disciples, "Let's go elsewhere"—to a rural provincial village. "I've come out for that." So they were to leave pretty lakeside Capernaum. There would be no two-week tent revival meeting. These Capernaumites were sufficiently fed. Jesus would not be captured by the popularity known in any one town. The two sets of fishermen brothers needed to learn that by weaning them from their hometown. Furthermore, perhaps Jesus did not want to risk this early in his ministry getting into a wrangle with the proud pedagogues of that handsome white limestone synagogue.

So they began a tour of Galilean villages. The fishermen not even missing their nets nor the rush of a day's catch, so focused were they on Jesus' teaching about repentance and life in his coming kingdom and on his ability to drive out devils. Learning, too, but not yet understanding fully: Jesus risks the inevitably crowd-pleasing spectacle of exorcism to touch the individual bound in miseries not entirely of his or her own schemes.

Touching the Unclean
A Man with Leprosy

A man with leprosy begged on his knees to be cured. . . . Jesus, touching
him, said, "Be clean. . . Tell no one. . . Show yourself to the priest. . . .
Keep Moses' law for cleansing." But the man published and blazed
abroad his cure. Jesus could not openly enter a town, so he stayed out in
the lonely desert places. —Mark 1:40-45

MARK IS A GREAT STYLIST AS A WRITER: clean, concise, brisk; the
voice elliptical, spare, selective. The latter qualities both endear
and frustrate the contemporary readers of his narrative. If Mark
is indeed writing in Rome, sixty years after the death of Jesus,
Roman sadists are his neighbors: Emperor Nero hung Christians, tar-pitched, on crosses, and at sundown burned them to
light up his suburban gardens. So the Greek-speaking assembly
of Christians, hiding, needed a brief narrative, an outline of the
Messiah's earthy life, to use for consolation and evangelism.

A modern reader finds curious the omission of a cured
leper's name—yet the inclusion of such a detail as "he begged on
his knees." Or is the significance not *who* but *what*. Too often
our analytically trained minds insist on authentication established by eye-witness and detailed fact: "Mr. Ezra Urriah Levy,
48, of Fish Lane, Bethsaida, was certified yesterday by Chief
Rabbi Moses Ben-Israel. . . ." But *who* is not the point; the focus
here is on a *what*—a cured leper!

Leprosy is known today as Hansen's disease, for Norwegian physician Armauer Hansen. Even if the descriptions (Lev. 13) seem more like psoriasis or shingles, let it be called leprosy! Who wants—like American athlete Lou Gehrig and English physician J. L. H. Downs—to have his name attached to a disease! Jesus' contemporaries knew the story of Miriam. Moses' eldest sister uttered a racial slur against Moses' Ethiopian wife, a remark that disclosed her rivalry for leadership.

God punished her, delaying the march to Zion with a week's worth of leprosy (Lev. 12). Thus, the disease was a punishment. Lepers were forced to live alone, expelled, perhaps not so much for medical reasons as religious. Their presence would contaminate the religiously orthodox.

So this leper, a desperate social outcast, begged on his knees for cleansing. And Jesus *touched* him, thereby making himself unclean. Quite early in his ministry is this foreshadowing of why he said, "I have come out for that." Jesus takes upon himself our leprosy—a leprosy today often not publicly noticeable as splotchy flesh and drunken brawls but a hidden canker. Ours a more refined evil, a discreet sin: character assassination, secretly plotted revenge, proud disbelief, deliberately withholding grace from our colleagues.

"I am willing," Jesus said, and acknowledged faith without first a theological or moral examination. No catechistic query. No: "Are you divorced and remarried? Are you a celibate homosexual? Are you a tax cheat?" Just: "Be clean!" But with a warning, a kind of odd "show and tell"—actually a *not* tell, but show. "Tell no one, but show the priest and keep the Mosaic law." Why does Jesus insist first on silence, then on accommodation to lawkeeping, he who himself will break as many as he will keep! Sometimes the best witness is silence and accommodation. One doesn't have to tell all to be honest; one doesn't have to break all conventions to be free in one's spirit.

But the man "went out and published and blazed abroad" (KJV) his healing. One can hardly condemn such exuberance. His new flesh radiant, he strode the marketplace, the water front, the country lanes, clad only in a loin cloth, the better to display the miracle of new flesh and a fresh set of hard abs. He's a hand-waving, Jesus-jumping charismatic, thinking only of his cleansed self, certainly not thinking at all of Jesus.

Already the Galilean towns mob this new preacher. Another healing—and one so astonishingly obvious—would draw larger crowds. Jesus knew well his people—an excitable, mercurial Jewish crowd could not be contained without force, and he would use none. They would keep him from the private touch on the individual—such as for Simon's mother-in-law, and this anonymous leper, now cavorting in religious ecstasy about the neighboring towns.

How hard it is for a naturally loquacious fellow to practice the Christian discipline of silence. He can even imagine his easy bubbling over of religious testimony as superior to his meditative, reflective, deliberate brother. He cannot see that too many words cheapen, make a good event dull, with the much repetition of hackneyed expressions of faith, of a religious code language: "born again," "saved," "God said to me." "I, I, I, I, I. . . . Blah! blah! blah!" can mar the witness to Christ one means to praise.

Because of this man, Jesus is driven again to the lonely place, the open country, the wilderness, the desert. The leper's much babbling about his encounter with Jesus drives Jesus away—from himself, from his neighbors. And the two sets of fishermen brothers learn from Jesus how false the claims: doing the will of the Father is full of joy; following Jesus is fun.

Just as the people did for John the Baptist down in the Judean countryside, so for Jesus; people came to him from all over the Galilean province. So much so that he is like Gerard Manley Hopkins' world which men "have trod, have trod, have trod. . . ." The people came and came and came. Yet, "for all this, (He) is never spent; / There lives the dearest freshness; deep down things" of his spirit abide."

Stupendous Stranger
Jesus Heals a Paralytic

Later Jesus came home to Capernaum. So many gathered, there was no room left, not even outside the door. . . . Four friends carried a paralytic. . . . Because of the crowd they dug an opening in the roof to let him down. When Jesus saw their faith, he said, "Son, your sins are forgiven. . . . Get up, take your mat and walk home."
—Mark 2:1-12

AFTER A COUPLE DAYS AND NIGHTS OUT in the lonely wilderness, Jesus risks returning to Simon's house. The villagers hear and again press in for fresh words from this astonishing teacher. "No room was left, not even outside the door."

If Simon's house was typical for Palestine, it contained the following, as any modern excavations of ancient sites reveal: an entrance hall, a storage room, bedrooms, a living room, a guest chamber, an open-walled courtyard, a flight or two of steps to a flat roof. In the low country and among the poor, the walls were of sun-baked mud brick, clay for mortar. The size of the family's fishing fleet suggests that Zebedee's sons could afford stone houses, common in larger towns. Still, here and now, no room.

Four men toting a paralytic friend in a litter were desperate to get him to this latest healer. These were not servants hired to lug a rich man from cure to cure. This was a labor of love. Friends happily carried their friend through the hot streets. But at the tight and excitable crowd, no one made room for them. That turned desperation into surliness. I imagine one of the blokes snarling, borrowing a line from Christopher Smart, "Where is this stupendous stranger?" They head for the flat roof, leaving me to think about this eighteenth-century British poet in my hymnal.

Why doesn't my congregation sing Smart's hymn? Could the director of music know that much of Christopher Smart's poetry was written during his seven-year period of religious dementia? Do they know of his "Jubilate Agno," where he asks us to consider his Cat Jeoffry? "For he is the servant of the Living God, duly and daily serving him. / . . . For he purrs in thankfulness when God tells him he's a good Cat. / For the divine spirit comes about his body to sustain it in complete cat"?

We should sing this song which begins in blustery belligerence: "Where is this stupendous stranger?" but ends with praise for the inexplicable mystery of God incarnate, "a native of the very world he made." Surely, it is something of this latter truth about Jesus that drove the four friends to tear up a roof.

We must not think of this roof as mere woven grass mats or bundles of dried rushes for shingles. Simon's was a stone house topped with solid stuff. Simon, a good Jew, would also have erected the obligatory wall about the edge of his roof, according to Deuteronomic law: "When you build a new house, make a parapet around your roof so that you may not bring the guilt of bloodshed on your house if someone falls from the roof" (22:8).

Let's not get distracted about the plaster grit falling into the mother-in-law's soup, which in later years will be known as French Onion. Nor should we worry about the destruction of property. Jesus rebuked no one for that. Indeed, his attitude suggests: Don't let property get in the way of meeting Jesus. A word we rich North American Christians need rubbed sorely into our accommodation to the soft Jesus of middle-class capitalism. Nor are we particularly interested in a paralytic.

Rather, like Jesus, our attention must center on the faith of the friends. (No mention is made of the paralytic's faith). We're shocked to discover that because of *their* faith, Jesus heals their friend. And learn here that it could happen that our own trust in God's goodness makes it possible for a sister, a friend, an uncle, a daughter to receive divine help. The faith of four friends helps their friend. Sins forgiven, legs snapped into place under him!

I am remembering an entry Henri Nouwen makes in his *Genesee Diary*. "God became flesh to show us that the way to come in touch with God's love is the human way, in which the limited and partial affection that people can give offers access to the unlimited and complete love that God has poured into the human heart. God's love cannot be found outside this human affection. . ." (36).

With the four friends of their paralytic buddy, I ponder that last declaration: only in human affection does one learn something of God's love. Their love for the friend brings him God's health. I do not know if that is the whole truth or good theology. But the love of others keeps bringing me to Christ.

And in another diary entry Nouwen records this confession to his spiritual director: we are troubled, on getting older, that our need for affection has not lessened. Fear that it might prevent rather than help the development of our spiritual life. His old saintly confessor noted that in our highly psychologized culture, reinforced by the media, being loved and giving love is all life is made out to be, as though there is nothing transcendental. That such highly nuanced psychological chatter makes the spiritual and theological language of love sound "irrelevant, superficial, and offensive." But divine love is more.

So, I come, in the end, to confess that my need for love is not solely for my own nurture but also to see, as did the four friends, God poured extravagantly, brazenly, freshly into young university men and women students. Looking on them, I am humbled to feel his eternal love rushing through me to them.

Matt Levy
The Calling of Levi

Once while Jesus walked by the lake and a crowd followed him, he began to teach them. Then he saw Levi sitting at the tax collector's booth. "Follow me," Jesus said. Levi got up and followed him. Later Jesus had dinner at Levi's house with tax collectors and sinners. . . . The Pharisees protested, "Why eat with these people?" —Mark 2:13-17

MATT LEVY SETTLED INTO HIS TAX-BOOTH that morning, abacus in hand, as he had done every day for twenty years. He had no reason to expect anything unusual was about to happen. The same old thing: wrangling with his Jewish people to collect money for the Roman colonizers of Palestine. Much of the work he relished; set his own hours, kept a long siesta, kept people waiting, set the rates, squeezed fat merchants for a bigger cut.

Little did he care that those nitpicking lawyers, the Pharisees, gave him wide berth and considered him an unpatriotic extortionist. "Tax collectors and sinners," those holy hypocrites always said of his job. Didn't care either that his own people considered him a collaborator with the enemy. He had to work, didn't he? Not all could go up to Jerusalem and take an M. Div. in esoteric snippets of the Talmud. And he didn't want to handle fish. They stank, plus the merest squall made him seasick.

It would be just another typical day. Josh with the tax collectors in the other booths: those collecting tariff on goods carried between cities, on produce brought into the village vegetable market, on caravans using the stone-paved Roman roads. Devise new schemes for entrapping the sleaziest of Shylocks. Pinch the bottoms of easy women peddling a heady wine. Had Matt Levy a radio, it would be tuned to Damascus; he liked the beat of that pagan rap. Anything was better than Radio Jerusalem with its whining rabbis and the religious schmaltz by the temple Glee Club. But it was not to be a typical day at his tax papers.

For out on the lake shore, Jesus strolled and talked again to the gathered crowd about life in his new kingdom. Granted, it was the same earlier crowd—the amazed, astounded, fickle and without-depth crowd, which in another three years would be yelling, "Crucify him!" True, the synagogue, the common place for daily religious discourse, was closing to Jesus because of his behavior (eating pork chops with lepers) and radical claims ("I have authority to forgive sins"). But he liked strolling on beaches with their fine winy air. So he strolled and taught, like a hundred other great rabbis, like the Greek philosophers, like a Chinese professor-poet at Yale.

Mark Salzman tells of meeting his Chinese poetry tutor twice a week: sometimes over tea, if the weather was bad; more often the two of them on long walks around New Haven. I too, in my own modest way at my non-Ivy League university, walked and talked with the rare student I'd allow an independent study in creative writing, fiction, or nonfiction. (Better they should take another lit course than get credit for writing, something they should do with passion, tempered and uncredited!) Indeed, such walks around Park View or talks over cappuccino in the Student Snack Shoppe proved a fine way for students to move discussions on rhetoric and persona to Nicodemus queries about faith and doubt, and to the glorious trivia of living: women, careers, parents.

When Jesus stepped into the shade for an iced tea and saw Matthew Levi, he said, "Follow me." Not only did Matt Levy follow, he took Jesus and his more intimate cluster of disciples home for dinner. He could well afford the meal, so he let the other curious tax collectors and sinners and some Pharisee lawyers also come along. An eclectic group for a dinner—the Pharisees, those self-righteous prigs, needing to be served by themselves at a table on the verandah. After all the work of setting up the separate table with her best china, only then did Ms. Levy discover that hoity-toity sect wouldn't even sit down to food in her house—a lot of good their notions about a bodily resurrection did to teach them manners! The social offscourings, "the people of the land"—as the Pharisees referred contemptuously to those who couldn't keep, not only all the Mosaic laws, but the ten thousand scribal laws—these crowded around Jesus and Matt Levy for mutton and leeks.

With all the chatter in his house, it never became clear to Matt Levy that day just what he had been called to do for this new rabbi. But some divine voice reached him where he longed to be touched with respect and affection. Later he was to learn Jesus' troupe needed a scribe, someone who would keep books until Judas Iscariot, that Judean, got his hands on the purse. Later too Matt Levy, now called Matthew, would write the most authoritative and comprehensive account of this Jesus. But that day he found it enough just to follow—crawl up from his soft camel-kid cushion, walk away at mid-life from a cushy career, not look back, not worry about rolling over his IRAs.

Following Jesus, then, wasn't much of an upward social climb for Matt Levy. He learned that the Pharisees were as contentious about Jesus as they had been contemptuous of tax collectors. He learned that he'd have to follow Jesus into more than just one unclean household and that he would need to break bread with the unwashed.

Following Jesus in his radical practice today still often offends those who are full of safe, conventional piety. Declaring that "Jesus did not come to call the righteous, but sinners," often hurts, but it is a precursor to spiritual health.

10

....

Oil and Wine
Jesus Is Questioned
About Fasting

Some people asked Jesus, "How is it your disciples aren't fasting?"...
Jesus answered, "How can the guests of the bridegroom fast?... No one
pours new wine into old wineskins. The new wine will burst the old
skin, and all is ruined. No, one pours new wine into new wineskins.
—Mark 2:18-22

LEAVE IT TO THE PHARISEES AND OTHER strict sects to hang a heavy
yoke on the simple people, those dumb oxen who plowed Judaism. Jehovah's commands to Moses included the requirement
of only one day of fasting a year (Lev. 16)—the Day of Atonement, or Yom Kippur. But by Jesus' time, strict Jews kept two
fast days a week—Mondays and Thursdays—6:00 to 6:00, from
sunrise to sunset. Many who kept those fast days touched up
their play-acting of penitence by streaking their faces with ash
and wearing worn weeds. But they would not stay at home; they
shuffled around town in a public display of their disheveled fasting. About them, Jesus once said, "I tell you the truth, they have
already received their reward in full."

This sunrise-to-sunset fasting of the Pharisees takes me back
to my years of living in Muslim Somalia, on the Horn of East
Africa. Practicing TOESL—the teaching of English as a second

language—before it had been invented as a respected discipline in language and literature departments of American universities put me in touch with young Mogadishu men on the eve of their nation's independence from Italy.

But our Christian mission closed its language schools during Ramadan, that ninth month of the Islamic year made sacred by daily fasting, obligatory for the orthodox. From dawn to dusk those orthodox students would not eat or drink or swallow saliva. So they spat on the floor, disgusting their Yankee teacher, or out the window, disrupting the lesson. Many of our classes were at night—when the men would eat a round of camel rump, rice pilaf, black Italian olives, and goat cheese, more important than learning about subjunctive conditionals of the World War II language of their British colonizers.

So the daily fast became a nightly feast, which rather blunted any high edge of respect I might have honed watching my students at their religious duties. Similarly the Jews of Jesus' time. During the day one could parade ashen piety; during the night one could stuff oneself with mutton, dates, and barley loaves. One could have it both ways: fast and feast.

Not only did my Muslim student friends fast. Years later, my wife's Catholic teacher colleagues kept a modicum of fasting during Lent—those forty days between Ash Wednesday and Easter. On Fridays they would eat no beef at lunch—no stroganoff or hamburgers. They grumbled about tuna sandwiches, which my African-born wife relished. For Lent, a few of her colleagues gave up smoking; near the end of the forty days they were irritable screamers in the classrooms. And still later, two soccer studs, British fiction students of mine, once told me they had sworn off masturbation during Lent.

The Christian discipline of fasting is a strange two-edged sword. We deny ourslves the things of pleasure (beef, chocolate, sex) for the sake of discipline, to prove we are masters of them. But oddly, the very denial of those objects heightens their enjoyment later. Ah! the bliss then of a naked Godiva chocolate on the tongue. Ah! the sweet release of pent up testosterone! Thus when fasting turns to feasting, we still must discipline ourselves, not allow gluttony.

Matt Levy's account of Jesus' words about fasting gives this additional warning and instruction: "When you fast, do not look somber as the hypocrites do, for they disfigure their faces to show men. . . . But when you fast, put oil on your head and wash your face, so that it will not be obvious to men that you are fasting, but only to your Father. . ." (6:16-18).

So, "guests of the bridegroom" are to sport new clothes, perfume their beards and gel-slick their hair, eat and drink, dance and sing songs full of romantic love and sexual innuendo, straight from Solomon's collection of "Jewish Folk Songs to be Sung at Rural Weddings." The wedding is to be a seven-day bash, a joyous occasion, a community festival. Jesus' coming to our spiritual party shatters all the old wineskins of conventional Jewish and denominational decorum.

He is the new wine in our new wineskins. While the Phoenicians might have glass bottles for their liquor, a new skin with its elasticity is just fine. No longer are we thin-skinned disciples, unduly susceptible to criticism, downright touchy and precious. Nor are we thick-skinned jerks, callous, insensitive to the dreams of our brothers and sisters. No longer are we like the Pharisees, or those dour old New England Puritans, of whom H. L. Mencken noted how unhappy they were if they thought that somewhere someone was having fun!

Ah! how to stay young in spirit, keep an open mind, welcome a new wine, I now in my mid-sixties, a creature of routine? When I felt myself a literary dinosaur among colleagues for whom "the question is no longer *what* the writer has written but rather *who* the writer is, what ethnic group or gender identity an author represents" (Francine Prose), and when I heard my young Anabaptist students say, "I love Madonna!" and thought of the Virgin instead of that ersatz screen version, I was happy to retire, to go away, to sip a wine mellow with age!

Grain and Whine
Lord of the Sabbath

One Sabbath Jesus and his disciples walking through grainfields picked some heads of grain. . . . The Pharisees said, "That's unlawful on the Sabbath.". . . Jesus said, "David and his hungry men ate the consecrated bread. . . . The Sabbath was made for man, not man for sabbath." —Mark 2:23-28

So what's "unlawful on the Sabbath"? Walking in a grainfield? Taking a neighbor's grain? Hand-threshing? Eating? Well, in this one episode just about everything Jesus and his disciples did was unlawful on the Sabbath!

The one sin they couldn't commit was stealing a neighbor's grain. The Law protected them: "If you enter your neighbor's grainfield, you may pick kernels with your hands, but you must not put a sickle to his standing grain" (Deut. 23:25). But the walking was suspect. A sabbath day's journey—assuming one was walking only to get to the synagogue or temple—allowed 2,000 cubits. With a cubit at about eighteen inches, that's 36,000 inches, 3,000 feet—or just over a half mile.

Jesus' troupe was hardly taking a short cut through a wheat field to get to the synagogue. Simon's house in Bethsaida was only blocks from the handsome white stone synagogue. So these Jesus People—these townsmen, teachers, tax collectors, and fishermen—were simply out on a Sunday afternoon stroll through the countryside. Something townspeople always like to do. Such strolls, full of nostalgia for childhood days of being down on the farm: working the soil and touching the livestock.

These village folk had been doing it all season: watching "first the blade and then the ear, then the full corn doth appear," ready for a taste-test. There in a ripening wheat field with the beneficent sun on their necks, no doubt the old promise of their Father God to their Father Noah after the flood rose to their minds: "As long as the earth endures, seedtime and harvest, cold and heat, summer and winter, day and night will never cease" (Gen. 8:22). But such strolling on the Sabbath was not allowed. Surely Jesus knew that! Yet there he was, breaking one of the scribal prohibitions.

By his time, the religious lawyers, the scribes, had thousands of rules and regulations concerning the Sabbath. It was not sufficient for God to have finger-etched into stone: "Remember the Sabbath Day; thou shalt not do any work." Religious lawyers had codified the behavior for a sabbath. According to William Barclay, "Work had been classified under thirty-nine different heads and four of these heads were: reaping, winnowing, threshing and preparing a meal."

Break off a few heads of wheat, rub them between your fingers, blow off the chaff, and pop the grain into your mouth—you've broken all four of the prohibitions! You feel dizzy—giddy, not with silly lightheartedness but with foolishly attempting not to break such scribal Sabbath laws.

But what is "work"? Do I work, pulling tender weeds Sunday afternoons, hidden from my neighbors by my rows of white pines and Russian olives? Many a lovely spring Sunday afternoon I took up the hoe and went happily into my garden of raised beds. After college teaching five days, a Saturday spent reading mind-numbing freshmen comps, and a Sunday morning's obligatory attempts at keeping public Protestant worship, I was glad when I said unto me, let us go into the garden of the Lord. Hidden from my neighbors, modern pagans and church-goers, I would work awhile, then, resting and waving my hoe over the spring-greening vegetable boxes, chant a line from Gerard Manley Hopkins:

> What would the world be, once bereft
> Of wet and of wildness? Let them be left,
> O let them be left, wildness and wet;
> *Long live the weeds* and the wilderness yet.

But this was not work, this was worship! Glad to be freed of my childhood's Old Testament keeping of Sabbath laws where only the cows got milked. And the discipline of my Puritan tribe, which prohibited afternoon "pleasure driving" through the countryside. Glad that the good Lord uttered an epigram: "The Sabbath was made for man, not man for the Sabbath"—women included! Glad for all that!

Yet not to disparage good work and the rest from it, I utter with the Psalmist-poet, "O Lord . . . establish Thou the work of our hands for us" (90:17). I acknowledge that I know this about work: good work gives me a stable psychological base, a social ethic, a way of reaching out to other people as a useful member of a community. Work demands that I renounce the search for purely selfish gratification. Thus work is a defense against hedonism and the loss of faith, against the powers of evil, against the self-absorbed despair which results from the vain pursuit of happiness, a right so quaintly enshrined in the Preamble to our nation's Declaration of Independence.

Thomas Carlyle, in *Sartor Resartus*, writes how an old Victorian professor learns the folly of the impossible imperative: "know thyself." For how shall one know oneself? The old Greek precept, Carlyle says, must translate itself into, "know what thou canst work at!" Indeed, when we have a choice, our work is not only a manifestation of our personalities, but more so of our values. Even of our worship.

It is hard to rest from that good work which makes all days Sabbath. Still we must let the day serve us: rest and worship.

More than an Ox in a Ditch
Lord of the Sabbath

In the synagogue there was a man with a shriveled hand. Some of them were looking for a reason to accuse Jesus, to see if he would heal on the Sabbath. . . . Jesus looked around at them in anger and, deeply distressed at their stubborn hearts, said to the man, "Stretch out your hand." —Mark 3:1-6

NO ONE COULD MISS THEM, SITTING in the front pews of the synagogue—these urbane members of the Sanhedrin—upper-middle class, Levites, all men, beards trimmed and perfumed with Oil of Moses. They strolled to the front with a suppleness borne of privilege and power, the suppleness of Blake's "tyger, tyger burning bright, in the forest of the night," leaving one in awe: What mortal hand or law dare frame such fearless synergy.

A rumor of an extraordinary rabbi up in Galilee teaching heresy had slammed through the religious courts of Jerusalem. A delegate of the Sanhedrin went grumbling up to investigate this rabbi who should have stayed by his lathe and planks instead of inciting the commoners with more good news.

They certainly had not come to be taught—not these aristocratic, imperialistic, ecclesiastical chaps. They were the chief judicial court, the Supreme Court of the Jews. The Rehnquist,

Scalia, Souter, Stevens, and more of the land (but without the Sandra Day O'Connors and Ruth Bader Ginsburgs!) They "came looking for a reason to accuse." They knew the law of Judea and of Rome. For them religion was ritual and fine old white limestone synagogues, like the one they sat in.

Ritual and fine old stone churches with stained light seemed to sum up why John Updike was still attracted to the Christian church. He sat talking to an assembly of wanna-be writers at Calvin College. Sophistication, decorum, a smile at the discreet lapse of human nature. Updike, while he liked ritual, would not have been a good member of the Sanhedrin. Those are more like my southern friend who shops at Jot and Tittles: attendance at Sunday's two church services, Wednesday Bible study, and prayer meeting, Thursday night choir practice, daily private devotions, family altar, and the sacred tithe of ten percent. Deep in the south, the practice of his faith is not tempered by the proximity of his lax northern brothers and sisters.

If you've come looking for a reason to accuse Jesus, you're not seeing the anonymous cripple, that recipient of controversial grace, of sudden health. The Greek suggests the "shriveled" hand was not one from birth but the damage a result of an accident. Tradition holds that the cripple was a stonemason, without workers' comp or disability. A good man; these years out of work, he didn't want to beg.

I like to think our stone mason worked on the limestone synagogue in which they all sat that morning for sabbath's rest. He went there often, knowing he'd receive nothing from the scribes and Pharisees, but the beautifully cut stone nourished him. He'd look up to the walls during the reading of the Torah. Two shaved stones set above a doorway looked as if they slept together instead of being shaped together. White, luminous limestone—yes, but with the blue veins in it, blue as lapis lazuli, "blue as a vein o'er the Madonna's Breast," as Robert Browning's old Bishop says of a stone while ordering his tomb at Saint Praxed's Church. Just such sensual love of stone, warm as a white breast with a blue, blue vein curling just by the rose nipple. Better our common stone mason studying the fine-cut synagogue stone, calling down its beauty, than a jealous old Renaissance bishop, drooling over peach blossom marble.

About Browning's poem, John Ruskin, nineteenth century historian and essayist, writes, "I know of no other piece of modern English, prose or poetry, in which there is so much told, as in these lines, of the Renaissance spirit—its worldliness, inconsistency, pride, hypocrisy, ignorance of itself, love of art, of luxury, and of good Latin. It is nearly all that I have said of the central Renaissance in thirty pages of the *Stones of Venice.*" Sounds, too, like a take on an up-scale Levite from Jerusalem.

As I said: no one could miss the assembled members of the Sanhedrin—even if they were few and not the seventy-one (Num. 11:16,17). Not everyone of them would want to take the donkey express eighty miles north to Capernaum to ferret out some rabble-rouser's blasphemy.

So Jesus saw a few of them sitting there that Sabbath. He deliberately precipitated a confrontation with authority. Perhaps the stone mason was a regular congregant; maybe Jesus had seen him before. The crippled arm was not life-threatening. Such care was allowed by a law which was not heartless—there is the ox-in-a-ditch-on-a-Sabbath thing. So Jesus "cut to the chase," as my non-fox-hunting colleague often said, irritated when we old men of the Language and Literature department accorded ourselves the privilege to ramble and recall. "Is it permitted to do good on the Sabbath?" That's the question.

"Stretch out your hand." Jesus' answer to his own question sets the keeping of a ritualistic religion against a religion of service, of spontaneous responses to people's needs. I once worked as a publicist for three years for a relief and service agency which, as a way of identifying its mission, carried on its letterhead, "A Christian resource for meeting human need." I rather liked signing my letters under such a wind-snapping banner. And would again, these thirty years later.

The Centuries Gyre
Crowds Follow Jesus

When people heard that Jesus was withdrawing to the lake, crowds came to him from Judea, Jerusalem, Idumea, from the regions of Transjordan and around Tyre and Sidon. To keep from getting crushed, Jesus told his disciples to prepare a small boat for him . When the evil spirits saw him, they cried out. —Mark 3:7-12

THE COMPRESSION OF MARK'S PROSE compares to Gerard Manley Hopkins' sonnets. The weight of centuries—Latin, Greek, Middle English—bear on a word or phrase, layering its connotative and denotative meanings, like the eons of vegetation pressed to make a seam of coal, the stress of carbon to lay a diamond. Mark's words are the "blue-bleak embers" of Hopkins' "The Windhover." Let such embers "fall, gall themselves," they'll "gash" open into "gold-vermilion."

Words, phrases, names, places, objects, time—all pile up, to get themselves lined up by a fine craftsman into one paragraph, concise, coherent, complete—yet teasing!

Each phrase is am ember waiting to spill out its compressed historical glow. Three examples: (1) "Jesus withdrew." If this God-Man needed to escape the press of his ministry is he establishing a principle: engage and retreat is the universal rhythm for a wholesome life? The diseased, like the poor, you have with you always? (2) "Have a small boat ready." Which of the fishermen disciples commandeered a boat from his father's fishing fleet? Was the morning's catch already in the fish market, the nets drying on the sand, the red boat beached and waiting to become a pulpit? (3) "Evil spirits cried out—but he gave strict orders not to tell who he was." They had already cried, "You are the Son of God." They cried a jubilato terrible to their own fate. Couldn't the people hear them? What language did they speak? Was it a spiritual tongue understood solely by Jesus?

Little Capernaum, always slightly cosmopolitan, a polyglot of tongues heard in its markets, had never seen anything like these last months. One might expect peoples from the far villages of the Galilean province to show up. But also from Judea, eighty to a hundred miles to the south? Including Jerusalemites? Peoples from Transjordan, those regions east of the river! Peoples from Tyre and Sidon, old Phoenician port cities on the Mediterranean! But it was the people from Idumea who sent me to my biblical geography and map books.

The slow study, the books closed now, the mind goes in spirals, following the history of leaders and peoples of old Idumea. Idumea, the Greek and Roman name for Edom, a territory which lies in the deep south, between the Dead Sea and the Gulf of Aqaba, on the western frontier of Arabia. Its capital was Petra, the blood-rose red city of rock. People that distant from Capernaum came to hear a new preacher in Galilee.

But first, it's back to the start with Esau's choice of land which he subdued, settled, grazed, married. His twin, Jacob, we follow into famine, Egyptian slavery, freedom, a forty-year uncharted wander with Moses in the Sinai. A later generation of these twins are destined to meet again in a region called Edom, old progenitor Esau's fiefdom now ruled by an ignorant king. Moses asked for permission to pass through their country. The old bad blood between brothers is loosed again. The request denied, the Israelite cousins flank their Esau cousins.

Later histories (the books of Samuel, the Chronicles of the Kings), favorable to the Israelites, tell of battles in the Valley of Salt, where David slew 10,000 and 18,000 Edomite men, until all Edom became subject to him. His son Solomon established a navy at Ezion Geber, today's Elath on the Gulf of Aqaba.

Minor prophets Amos, Joel, and Obadiah thundered against Edom, predicting it would become a wasteland. After the exile, the Israelites came home to find the Edomites pressed into their southern towns, even Hebron, by the Nabataean Arabs. Still later, with Rome in a battle against Jerusalem, the Israelites accept an offer of 20,000 Edomites into the Holy City to help defend it. Once inside the gates, they turned traitor and slew their distant cousins, according to Josephus. When Jerusalem fell, the Romans did likewise to the Edomites.

Some men from Edom/Idumea were among those who crushed Jesus into a boat. Centuries and centuries later, here on a lake shore, the sons of Esau met the Prince of Jacob! I feel giddy with the rush of such spiralings of histories. Lines from Yeats' "Second Coming" swirl in my head, but with an opposite spin. "Turning and turning in a closing gyre," the Edomites hear too Christ-the-Falconer! Things fall together? Esau's anarchy loosed upon the earth, his blood-dimmed tide of violence, washed against waters of a guileless Galilean Teacher. We know it will be no rough beast, but a lamb, not slouching, but walking to Jerusalem, not to be born, but to die.

It is another Epiphany—another proclamation of the good news to the Gentiles, beyond that first in a straw stable to three old wise men. Another proclamation, to the Edomites of his day: "You have heard it said: 'Jacob have I loved, but Esau have I hated!' (Mal. 1:1, 2). But I say: 'Come to the Waters!'" A Son dares to break his father's old curse!

To the Edomites of his day and the Edomites of our day, he says, "You live among a people who do not believe in the transcendent God, who say there is no grace, only genetic juice and environmental conditioning—scientific determinism. But I say: Come to the Waters, O taste and see! Indeed, taste it again, grace, for the first time!" And I did sit and drink.

Called to be Sent
The Appointing of the
Twelve Apostles

Jesus went up on a mountainside and called to him those he wanted, and they came to him. He appointed twelve—designating them apostles—that they might be with him and that he might send them out to preach. . . . —Mark 3:13-19

From seaside to mountainside. Mark leaves to our imagination just how this shift of scene came about. How did he extricate a dozen men from a dozen- thousand crowd? Was it with a tap on the shoulder and a whisper in the ear that he told the place to rendezvous? Was it in code: "Altarwise at owl-light," and they knew where to scramble? Was it in the small boat he had earlier in the day ordered ready (3:9)? More likely this retreat to a mountainside did not follow the day after the seaside crush and a sermon from the boat.

We read of four fishermen and one tax-collector being called. Now quite suddenly there are twelve. Surely as Jesus walked through the cornfields and on the seashore, he kept his eye out for a few other young men in their late twenties and early thirties, men his peers. These next seven who were to receive their apostleship also felt the magnetism of Jesus; they could not explain their being possessed by a power, sudden and extraordinary, which aligned the rough filings of their iron psyche to a

Magnetic Pole outside of themselves. These too felt a curiously intimate electrical current running between themselves and Jesus. They felt the Call.

I can imagine this calling of the twelve quite differently. "Jesus went up on a mountainside" alone. In the early evening he saw a small boy and a few sheep dropping down from grazing in the high green hills, returning to the village fold for the night. Of this kid Jesus asked, "Do you know a big noisy fisherman called Simon?"

Surely, everyone knew Simon, the boy laughed.

"Be a good son; go find Simon and tell him, 'Jesus is calling you. You'll find me on Mole Hill.'" Simon would know where Jesus awaited him; they had been there often, particularly when the cured leper blabbed his healing so much that Jesus couldn't risk entering a town openly. He stayed outside in lonely places, his only companion Simon. Now, the call would come again to that sturdy fisherman.

"He called to him those he wanted." Simon came with a rush of wild beard and cloaks, happy, needed. Jesus then sent him back to town with the same message for James, the oldest son of Thunder: "Jesus is calling you." Finding Jim, Pete returns to Jesus. The Rabbi then sent James down to the village to find his brother John with the same message: "Jesus is calling you." And so on, singly, each man receiving the call—until Simon the Zealot fetched Judas Iscariot, the twelfth man.

Four former fishermen, a reformed tax collector, and an ex-political guerrilla—about the careers of the other six we know nothing. No one of great wealth or great social prestige; no theologian or philosopher—in fact, perhaps not all of them could read. An odd lot of fellows to say yes to one rabbi, whose teachings already had gotten them into a heck of a lot of trouble with orthodox Jewry.

Answering "I will follow," they could not have known they'd spend three years together, that their leader would be killed, their group disintegrate. That they themselves would be flung out into the whole world, to teach, suffer, die. Crucified in Rome,

Jerusalem, Egypt, Persia, Ethiopia—by the sword, by the arrow, by flaying, according to historical documents and traditional stories. Only John and Philip would die natural deaths. One would commit suicide, in deep grief over betrayal and collaboration with the temple and the Palace. It was to be a wild ride with their saying "Yes" to Jesus' call—this special call that went only to "those he wanted."

We need not torment ourselves with a fanciful question: Would I have answered that call? Nor, I suppose, need we torment ourselves with the darker observation: Since our names are not listed, we are among the uncalled. That was then; this is now.

"Come unto me all you who are weary and heavily laden" still comes, if not from the Rabbi's special mountainside retreat, then from the Voice above the chatter of the seaside throng. We too are "a chosen people. . . called out of darkness into his wonderful light. Once we were not a people, but now we are the people of God. . ." (1 Pet. 2: 9). These words written "to God's elect, scattered throughout Pontus, Galatia, Cappadocia, Asia and Bithynia," and North America—written from an ox-like fisherman, one Simon now Peter, who was the first of twelve to receive the Apostolic call.

Rather than cloak himself in scarlet and ermine and enthrone himself on a high gold chair—because of his remarkable charismatic leadership; because of the high esteem in which he was held for his missionary travels and hardships; because he was to die a martyr in Rome, crucified upside down on request (according to Tertullian), not feeling himself worthy to mirror his Lord's death—Simon Peter would have none of that pomp. Rather, this man of special calling to apostleship, himself turned and *called all peoples* into Christ's Commonwealth.

Still, today, one feels with George Herbert this call in his poem, "Love."

> Love bade me welcome: yet my soul drew back. . .
> And know you not, sayes Love, who bore the blame? . . .
> You must sit downe, sayes Love, and taste my meat:
> So I did sit and eat.

Lord of the Flies
Jesus and Beelzebub

Teachers of the law from Jerusalem said, "He is possessed by Beelzebub! By the prince of demons he drives out demons." Jesus said, "How can Satan drive out Satan? . . . A house divided against itself cannot stand. . . . Whoever blasphemes against the Holy Spirit will never be forgiven." —Mark 3: 22-30

What a panoply of devils! The doctors of jurisprudence, starched and impeccably dressed ethicists, hurling names at Jesus, named themselves. *Beelzebub*, a term borrowed from a Philistine tongue, literally meaning "Lord of the Flies." *Satan*, the adversary. *Devil,* the accuser. *Demon,* daemon, daimonion, an evil spirit. *Belial,* child of wickedness. *Lucifer,* a morning star, a lightbringer, now fallen, a rebel archangel. *Evil,* a malignancy which infests the world, its people, and its systems. Thus in opposition to the Good. Such a panoply of devils carries my mind to the devils of literature I have read and taught for three decades:

One is Chillingworth, the cold, intellectual scientist who probes the Reverend Dimmesdale's heart in Hawthorne's *The Scarlet Letter.* The doctor knows "the spring that controlled the engine" of the minister's nature. He brings "a terrible machinery to bear" upon his patient's heart. He "tampers with the delicate springs" of the reverend's mind and conscience. Chillingworth comes to embody that evil science which penetrates, exposes, and reduces to its own terms the experiences of religious faith—the detached intellectual's query without compassion.

Another devil is Claggart, the evil master-at-arms who destroys the innocent *Billy Budd* of Melville's novel. The psychological motivation for the destruction is no better explained than in lines from W. H. Auden's poem, "Herman Melville":

> Evil is unspectacular and always human,
> And shares our bed and eats at our own table.
> And we are introduced to Goodness every day,
> Even in drawing-rooms among a crowd of faults;
> He has a name like Billy and is almost perfect
> But wears a stammer like a decoration:
> And every time they meet the same thing has to happen;
> It is Evil that is helpless like a lover
> And has to pick a quarrel and succeeds,
> And both are openly destroyed before our eyes.

A third devil is Mr. Kurtz, that "emissary of pity, and science, and progress" in Conrad's *The Heart of Darkness*. Far upriver on an interior ivory-collecting station, alone in the wilderness, "where no warning voice of a kind neighbor would be heard," he loses grip on his Victorian restraint, "his soul looks into itself . . . and goes mad."

Mr. Kurtz—"all Europe contributed to the making of him"—could write seventeen pages of rhapsodic prose in praise of colonialism ("mostly means the taking away from those who have a different complexion or slightly flatter noses than ourselves, not a pretty thing when you look into it too much"). Mr. Kurtz begins with this sentence: "By the simple exercise of our will we can exert a power for good practically unbounded. . . ." but ends with the terrifying postscript: "Exterminate all the brutes!"

We learn from history: the Spanish Inquisition, the Anabaptist martyrdom, the German Holocaust, the American architects of the Vietnam war—by the same "exercise of will we can exert a power for EVIL practically unbounded."

A fourth devil, the Grand Inquisitor, having captured Jesus on a visit to sixteenth-century Seville, admits, "We have taken the sword of Caesar, and in taking it, of course, have rejected Thee and followed him. . . . We tell them [the common folk] that every sin will be atoned, if it is done with our permission. . . . I have joined the ranks of those who have corrected Thy work. . . . If anyone has deserved our fires, it is Thou. Tomorrow I shall burn Thee. . . ." For Ivan, the intellectual with a brilliant analytical mind in Dostoyevsky's *The Brothers Karamazov* , this kind of evil, this kind of torture, compounded with the torture of innocent children, nurtures in him atheism and eventually insanity, so horrible is such human corruption.

Then, too, there is the whole panoply of Shakespeare's evil characters, from Mr. and Mrs. Macbeth to Iago. Evil resides not only in great literature but seems inherent in the very existence of a human world. "It is men [and women], not God, who have produced racks, whips, prisons, slavery, guns, bayonets, and bombs; it is by human avarice or human stupidity, not by the churlishness of nature, that we have poverty and overwork" (89), writes C. S. Lewis in *The Problem of Pain.*

One sees people "possessed by an evil spirit" on any evening's news: A man chained and dragged to death behind a pickup truck. A newborn baby fried in a microwave. The CEO of a highly productive industrial giant awarded a share of stock that makes him worth 300 times more than his janitor. Rwanda, Kosovo, East Timor. With evil so prevalent, one joins M. Scott Peck's query in *People of the Lie*: with evil central to religious thought for millenia, how is it that the concept of evil "is virtually absent from our science of psychology?" The good doctor attempts some definitions of the psychic malignancy: "Evil is that which opposes the life force." And "Evil is defined as the use of power to destroy the spiritual growth of others for the purpose of defending and preserving the integrity of our own sick selves" (119).

Just now I can think of no better explanation for the behavior of the doctors of religious jurisprudence flinging epithets at Jesus. He had cut them to the quick.

Brothers and Friends Jesus' Mother and Brothers

When his family heard, they went to take charge of him (Jesus). "He's out of his mind." When they arrived, they sent someone through the crowd to Jesus. "Your mother and brothers are outside looking for you." He asked: "Who are my mother and my brothers?" Then he looked at those seated with him: "Here—whoever does God's will is my brother and sister and mother." —Mark 3:20,21,31-34

FOR MONTHS NOW, RUMORS HAD DRIFTED home to Nazareth. Rumors about her eldest son, their eldest brother, getting mixed up in seething crowds, exorcisms, nasty debates with the synagogue fathers, and making claims for himself that sounded like religious dementia. Plus a nasty bit of gossip about giggly loose women. It was time for Mother Mary and the four brothers (the sisters would stay at home) to go get Jesus, "to take charge of him."

Jesus was becoming an embarrassment to his family. Not only did he not stay by his father's vocation—what's so demeaning about turning out a handsome Duncan Phyfe leg for a table? Can't one take pride in lining a blanket closet with mellow rose cedar?—he called others away from their family businesses. And his first sermon in their hometown synagogue still rankled his brothers. All four—James, Joseph, Simon, Judas—went with pride, no trepidation—to hear their eldest brother preach his maiden sermon. Reading from Isaiah: "The Spirit of the Lord is on me. . . to proclaim the year of the Lord's favor," Jesus sat down to teach and had the cheek to make the most audacious declaration: "Today this Scripture is fulfilled in your hearing" (Luke 4: 16-30). Time to bring him back to the carpentry shop.

Not only does this son/brother not come out to receive his kin, offer them a cup of cold water, bathe their dusty feet, they hear offensive words clapped above their heads from his lips. "Mother? brother?—who're they? You, and whoever does God's will." This utterance rings of a truth his family could not yet absorb. Thus the emotional cost to child and parent and siblings is high. Even if we console ourselves with the facts: Jesus is no seventeen-year-old drifter, bored with boards and saws; he's a thirty-year-old man, getting a late start on his mission. Possibly he had worked as bread-winner, turning out stools and cupboards in the family cabinet shop, after the death of his father, until the four younger brothers could take over. Still, we parents feel the sting of such callous dismissal by a blood-relative.

I cannot keep from flipping ahead in Mark's narrative and the other gospels. I want reconciliation between eldest son and his family. I find it in his mother's visit to the crucifixion scene, in the son's arrangement for her care. After the Ascension, Mary and the brothers are listed as present in an upstairs room along with the confused disciples, "joined in prayer" (Acts l:14). After the resurrection brother James not only worshiped Jesus as the Christ but became the head of the church in Jerusalem. Later, when the Jesus gospel swept Gentiles from around the Mediterranean into the new Christian fellowship, the contentious issue of keeping circumcision arose. It was James—perhaps now Bishop James—who drew up a letter releasing Gentile Christian from this Jewish "yoke," as Peter described it.

But such reconciliation is three years away. Now the question is this: Do we need mother and brothers? We've had a call—from where there is need, from that which "makes us the gladest," as Frederick Buechner puts in it *The Hungering Dark-*

ness. We may discover that to be free to answer such a vocational call, mother and brothers cannot, should not, travel with us. They are not adequately equipped.

They can stand and wave goodbye as we take journey into that other country—physically, vocationally, emotionally, intellectually, even spiritually. But other than their prayerful best wishes, there's little mother and brothers can give us.

Our new place will differ greatly from the familiar rounds of the hometown family carpentry shop. We'll need to find other mothers, other brothers.

I found just such a mother in Somalia, when I first went to East Africa fresh out of college, forty years ago. Martha Keener, the age of my mother, disciplined me with an authority I could respect. Educated, an old experienced teacher in crosscultural, cross-religious milieu, Aunt Martha could aid me to adapt to conditions of teaching in a Muslim, Italian-colonial assignment in a manner my mother could not. Not to discredit my mother, but for all her love and concern for me, she could not enter into my new life; her life as farm wife and later as wife to a small town merchant, limited her.

Later, it would be similarly true of my blood-brothers. How different are those good men—farmers, businessmen—from my professional colleagues, my new brothers. Our common interests in literature, in the college classroom, bred an intellectual camaraderie for fencing with one's wits, sprung from a literary life: libraries, books, words. A life needing solitude and reflection for spiritual poise.

Still later, a younger set of brothers—some few of my former students—carry me along on the current of their lives, with a grace and sustenance my older blood brothers cannot. For, it is as C. S. Lewis says in *Four Loves*, "If we [university profs] are any good we must always be working toward the moment at which our pupils are fit to become our critics and rivals. We should be delighted when it arrives. . . ." So sometimes it must be that we need to find other mothers, other brothers. And if there is a need, await the reconciliation with kin; it will come.

The Efficacy of Story
The Parable of the Sower

Again Jesus began to teach by the lake. Because of the crowds he got into a boat and sat in it out on the lake, while all the people were along the shore. He taught many things by parables. "Listen! A farmer went out to sow his seed. . . . Seed sown on good soil, produces a crop. . . ."
—Mark 4:1-20

JESUS TOOK HIS TEACHING OUTSIDE OF THE synagogue. He shifted from lake to mountain to house. Then again: "Once more to the lake." Here, something new came into his teaching: the parable. I do not mean to suggest that Jesus invented a literary genre. No! Rather, his employing parables is new to his Galilean ministry. His audience was familiar enough with the form, hearing old rabbis use it often to illustrate a moral precept. Yet, curiously, biblical literary scholars and the eminent authorities of my *Harper's Bible Dictionary* insist that in the Old Testament there are only *two* parables: Nathan's story to King David about a poor man with one lamb (2 Sam. 12:1-14); and Isaiah's parable of the unproductive vineyard (5:1-7).

Further, the eminent authorities warn against confusing the parable with fable, allegory, myth, extended metaphors. Yet one eminent authority declares this parable of the sower and the seed to be just that: an allegory. Like Edmund Spenser's *The Faeire Queene*, a literary horror to any but one of an antique mind; like

John Bunyan's *Pilgrim's Progress,* "the most successful allegory in our English literature," warbles one editor of the Norton Anthology.

Thus: as with seeds in the soil, so were the words of Jesus in the hearts of his hearers. He who has ears, let him hear! While the sun dries up seeds in a rocky place. While thorns choke out some seed. Still, always, there is good soil which receives seed from the sower: it yields an abundant crop; there is joy at harvest time!

I cannot read (or write) about this parable and not turn once more to study the Van Gogh print of "The Sower" hanging on the wall behind my head. With its thick color, its flickering and pulsing landscape, no one would mistake it for the Monet gardens and lily pond at Giverny. Here, the fertile soil is open and fluid as water. The dark sower wears the massive sun as halo. The thick tree trunk slants to soil and sun and sower. But this is not the rural romanticism of a John Constable's *The Hay Wain* (wagon), nor the calm lives of Peter Bruegel the Elder's peasants at their planting, harvesting, and haymaking. A darkness broods over van Gogh's landscape. I want the "Crows over Wheatfield" to flap into this painting, want their hint of malignancy to undulate over the land. Let them be the birds that swoop to snatch up the seed in Jesus' parable.

But back to written parable, not painted ones. Not only did ancient rabbis employ the parable. So did the early church fathers, perhaps none so well as the fourth century desert saints of Egypt, Arabia, and Palestine. Like their Jesus, rather than give an abstract theological discourse, say, on the atonement, they preferred to tell a concrete story. One from Thomas Merton's *The Wisdom of the Desert* will handsomely illustrate the power of narrative.

"A certain brother came to Abbot Silvanus at Mount Sinai, and seeing the hermits at work he exclaimed: Why do you work for the bread that perisheth? Mary has chosen the best part, namely to sit at the feet of the Lord without working. Then the Abbot said to his disciple Zachary: Give the brother a book and let him read, and put him in an empty cell.

"At the ninth hour the brother who was reading began to look out to see if the Abbot was not going to call him to dinner, and sometime after the ninth hour he went himself to the Abbot and said: Did the brethren not eat today, Father? Oh yes, certainly, said the Abbot, they just had dinner. Well, said the brother, why did you not call me? You are a spiritual man, said the elder, you don't need this food that perisheth. We have to work, but you have chosen the best part. You read all day, and get along without food. Hearing this the brother said: Forgive me, Father. And the elder said: Martha is necessary to Mary, for it was because Martha worked that Mary was able to be praised" (36-37).

Such a story surely checks any Christian at his contemplative best from sliding toward narcissism or spiritual megalomania. As even does the wise teaching of Conrad's *Heart of Darkness* by any Judeo-Christian university prof.

Remember the novel's framing device? Conrad writes a story about a fellow named Marlow who tells of his adventure up the Congo River to four listeners: a lawyer, an accountant, a company director, and the unnamed narrator of the tale. While concentrating on his own moral education, Marlow tries to get his listeners to recognize their own complicity with all the forces of destruction described in the story about a corrupted Mr. Kurtz; "all Europe contributed to the making of him."

So how many listeners respond to Marlow's story? Only the unnamed narrator recognizes and responds appropriately. The lawyer, accountant, and director are those whom Jesus describes: "They are like seed sown among thorns; they hear the word: but the worries of this life, the deceitfulness of wealth and the desires for other things come in and choke the word, making it unfruitful."

Thus, we delight in Jesus' use of story. For he, like Conrad, demonstrates his faith in the "moral efficacy" of experience through literature. So, let the Christian read fiction—good stories, long novels—for all great literature is moral by nature.

The Pith of Epigram
Four Sayings of Jesus

Jesus said to them: "Don't put a lamp under a bed, but on a stand.
Everything done in secret will be revealed. The measure you use is the
measure you'll receive. Whoever has will be given more; whoever lacks,
it will be taken away." —Mark 4:21-25

EMPLOYING EPIGRAMS, JESUS, THE GREATEST teacher of the New Testament imitates the greatest teacher of the Old Testament, King
Solomon. (But just as an aside, an admission of a problem in
naming Solomon: never understood how one could be so wise
and be such a fool about women. One look at three thousand
pairs of panty hose drying in his bathroom should have reined in
the testosterone surges!) Yet, this teacher was full of wise sayings;
I make no nice literary distinctions between an aphorism: a concise statement of principle; an epigram: a terse, witty, often paradoxical saying; a proverb: a popular saying; and an adage: a
saying often metaphorical in form that embodies a common observation. A few to illustrate:

"Drink water from your own cistern, running water from
your own well" (Prov. 5:15). "Go to the ant, you sluggard; consider its ways and be wise!" (Prov. 6:6). Old Aunt Martha from
my youthful Somalia days has pinned in my mind forever her interpretation of that proverb with her own brand of whimsical
wisdom. "The only thing I learn from a study of ants is that they

take time to go to all the picnics!" And Proverbs 26:1: "Like snow in summer or rain in harvest, honor is not fitting for a fool."

Many of the desert fathers and mothers got themselves remembered for uttering aphorisms. Abbot Pastor said, "Any trial whatever that comes to you can be conquered by silence." And: "Do not dwell in a place where you see that others are envious of you, for you will not grow there."

Accompanying these saintly makers of epigrams are also Milton, Pope, Keats, Ben Franklin. "The mind is its own place, and in itself / Can make a Heav'n of Hell, a Hell of Heav'n"—*Paradise Lost.* "Hope springs eternal in the human breast"—*An Essay on Man.* And "True wit is nature to advantage dressed, / What oft was thought, but ne'er so well expressed"—*An Essay on Criticism.* "Beauty is truth, truth beauty—that is all / Ye know on earth, and all ye need to know"—*Ode on a Grecian Urn.* Finally *Sayings of Poor Richard*: "Experience keeps a dear school, but a fool will learn in no other." "Love your neighbor; yet don't pull down your hedge." "Fish and visitors smell in three days."

Whether amorous, elegiac, meditative, complimentary, satiric, polished, terse, pointed or witty, the epigram is not one of my favorite literary devices. Listed, their subjects keep jumping, irritatingly. A bit like reading the dictionary. Just now mine lies open to a column of "p" words: "penicillium, peninsula, penis, penitence, penitentiary, penknife, pennant, penniless, Pennsylvania Dutch. . . ." And so on, which makes for a jumpy read. I don't even like my own witticisms remembered.

Former students returning to their alma mater for homecoming weekend, and finding me among the stuff, exclaim a decade later, "Oh, I'll never forget what you once said in British fiction." My affectionate gaze on seeing them goes rigid with worry. Then I hear myself cited: "I'm getting quite good at cloaking my first brushes with senility as eccentricity!" Or: "We chose to attend Weavers Church because we wanted our children to know that one can be a Republican and still get in to heaven!"

Summarizing epigrams may seem silly—they're so condensed to begin with—yet these four by Jesus touch on a great truth: hearing his teaching without responding, one is in danger of losing ownership even of a slight divine truth. For example: "Don't put a light under a bed," Jesus said. (And I say unto you: "Or you'll burn your mattress!") The greater wisdom here has something to do with truth needing to be seen. Our faith is meant to be displayed. Matthew's context for this proverb adds Jesus' further injunction: "In the same way, let your light shine before men, that they may see your good deeds and praise your Father in heaven" (Matt. 5:16).

Isn't it a lack of prudence or caution—to flare out one's good works? Even *Ad Majoreum Dei Gloriam* ("To the Great Glory of God")? Yes, even when such public displays mean martyrdom: the first Christians of Rome; the first Anabaptists of Luther's Germany.

Yet I must confess to a slight resistance to this public display of my lighted lamp. Not false modesty, I hope, but some deeply entrenched sense of decorum. Such as C. S. Lewis touches on in his "The Weight of Glory" sermon:

"Glory suggests two ideas to me, of which one seems wicked and the other ridiculous. Either glory means to me fame, or it means luminosity. As for the first, since to be famous means to be better known than other people, the desire for fame appears to me a competitive passion and therefore of hell rather than heaven. As for the second, *who wishes to become a kind of living electric light bulb?*" (8, italics mine).

Who indeed! Little wonder then that St. Paul once coined the phrase "the eternal weight of glory" to describe the Shekinah glow that awaits the Christian after his "light and momentary troubles" (2 Cor. 4:5). So, let the light shine from Jesus' epigrams, witty and profound, satiric and paradoxical. And I shall try to dwell in their glow—without self-consciousness, without embarrassment.

Seed-Time and Harvest
Two Parables About Seed

Jesus said, "This is what the kingdom of God is like. A man scatters seed . . . and all by itself the soil produces grain. . . : like the smallest mustard seed, which grows to the largest of all garden plants."
—Mark 4:26-29; 30-34

I'VE BEEN PLANTING WILD FLOWER SEEDS this fall, from a pound bag which holds, in order of predominance, bachelor button, scarlet flax, painted daisy, blue flax, rocket larkspur, candytuft, gypsophila, sweet alyssum, baby blue eyes, siberian wallflower, lupin, mixed California poppy, clarkia, corn poppy, purple coneflower, black-eyed susan, plain coreopsis, sweet William, dame's rocket, spurred snapdragon, catchfly, bird's eye, gaillardia, Chinese houses, yarrow, white floxglove, and columbine.

I stood in the golden slant-light of early October and read flower names aloud over the prepared soil. Like Adam speaking their names into existence, I hoped they would respond to the summons locked in their tiny, tiny seeds—some surely as tiny as the proverbial mustard seed—and spring to paint the slope under the apple trees next May. Like the dumb farmer of Jesus' parable, I don't know how this happens. Like him too, whether I "sleep or get up," whether I brood over Faulkner or brood over the soil, these wild flower seeds, "all by themselves produce" wild flowers, each after her own kind.

Dumber than the farmer in Jesus' parable, who could at least identify grain seed: rye, wheat, barley, millet—I can't identify by seed even one of the flowers-to-be in my palm. So, I have to trust the seed merchant and his labeling—and read again the lovely sounds on his packet of wild flowers: bachelor button, scarlet flax, painted daily, blue flax, rocket larkspur, and on and on, a litany of holy names, these seeds the extravagant squander of a profligate God!

I need to trust, too, the label that declares only .01 percent of the package weight is "other crop"—of what? Spinaches and radishes, tares and mustard? And what's in the .01 percent "weed seed" in my pound packet? I pray it is not ragweed, crabgrass, or dandelion—sufficient unto the season is their evil thereof.

I wonder, too, about the "bloomcoat" of colors painted on these seeds: oranges, blues, greens, the dominant. Are they sprayed with a protective nasty-tasting-coating—something to deter the grackles, those hard, yellow-eyed fellows that spiral up like so many black seeds flung into the clear air every fall above my garden and land and chitter and strut and peck and would steal my wild flower seeds?

Across the country road my Old Order Mennonite neighbor farmer these October days drills rye into his no-tilled soil. But in that field will be no "first the blade, then the ear, then the full grain doth appear." His rye is a winter crop for putting nutrients in the soil, but to be poisoned by herbicides in the spring; into those blanched fields he will plant corn, year after year. I squelch the worry as to which generation hence will produce two-headed calves, three-legged boys, tumorous cancers growing secretly in my well water. Rather, it's back to sowing a seed whose secret growth is like the kingdom of God.

I like the organic imagery of Jesus' parable: the kingdom seed is planted; hidden it grows, day and night, until, as Dylan Thomas sings, "the force that through the green fuse drives the flower," the rye, the mustard seed. And we farmers, playful and earnest, are "happy as the grass is green!" After "the blade, then the ear, then the full corn doth appear;" and "we put the sickle to it."

The kingdom of God/the kingdom of heaven—even the most avid defender of the glorious Davidic kingdom had also to acknowledge a civil war which led to two kingdoms, disastrous alliances with foreign kings, rebellions, stupid military tactics, waywardness from their Jehovah-God. Their whole sorry history is about the collapse of an attempt to found a Hebrew kingdom. They never came close to establishing an equitable common-wealth, a *shalom* of social, material, and spiritual health. Now, under Roman rule, the saintly await a spiritual kingdom, the nationalists, a political solution.

But Jesus tells the crowds about a new kingdom of God which begins with himself, now, in politically smitten Palestine, and will go on until "some from every tribe and nation and peoples" will come in and salute him and his Father-God as the beneficent architects of a new order.

And we are fools if we believe that the fullest expression of this new Jesus Kingdom is solely our own human struggle for social and material betterment, for peace and restorative justice. Apart from the worship of a transcendent God and from the power of his holy presence in human affairs, our little social and political engines will have their day, then sputter. Our post-Jesus era of human history is full of debtors' prisons, child labor, urban squalor, war, slavery, bigotry, economic disparity. But still the Christian worked, engaged in the agendas of her or his society. And our post-industrial revolution is also full of the hard labor of good men and women in triumph against the evils of despotism, political, clerical, and economic.

Still to this transcendent Christ, the Christian prays: "Thy kingdom come; thy will be done, on earth as it is in heaven." Amen. So be it!

Asleep in the Stern
Jesus Calms the Storm

When evening came they crossed to the other side of the lake. Leaving the crowd behind, they took Jesus along, just as he was, in the boat. There were also other boats with him. A furious squall came up, waves broke over the boat; it nearly swamped. Jesus was in the stern, sleeping on a cushion. The disciples woke him. "Teacher, don't you care if we drown?" He got up and rebuked the wind and waves. Then he rebuked his disciples. "Why are you so afraid?" Still terrified they said to each other, "Who is this man?"—Mark 4:35-41

IT'S THE DETAILS OF THIS STORY THAT DISTRACT me this morning: leaving the crowd behind; took Jesus just as he was; the other side; the other boats; the cushion. Heard enough sermons on: Jesus, master of nature; Jesus, also wearied from work; Jesus, in my boat. I'll row into the vivid details.

Leaving the crowd behind. I find here reassurance that I did it right when I'd say to my two sections of Freshman Comp every fall: "Don't call me at home. I don't bother you after 5:00 o'clock; you shouldn't bother me!" Leave behind freshman (Yes, I know the politically correct phrase to avoid offense to the two-females-to-every-one-male: "first-year students")—and their soggy essays; go over the hills west of my little university into the evening sun—"tired but happy"—to coin a cliché. After a day in the Lord's vineyard, slashing out purple passages, tying up branches of dangling modifiers, snapping off suckers of comma splices, I too would leave the crowd behind. Freshmen Comps, like the poor, like the diseased, you have with you always. I needed to turn to something else for nourishment, if only a rereading of Gide's *The Immoralist*, or Cheikh Hamidou Kane's *Ambiguous Adventure*. But none of the Eighteenth Century writers, reasonable or mad. Not everything rejuvenates!

Over to the other side. The opposite shore of Lake Galilee puts one among the Gerasenes, residents of one of the cities of Decapolis, a rather non-Hebrew territory. Jesus went there for some R&R. When I stood on the eastern shore and looked across that lake, it was only weeks after the 1967 "Seven Day War." The other side—the Syrian Golan Heights—bristled with Israeli artillery. It did not seem just then a place for a timorous tourist. But back home, once in awhile when I've had all I can take of piety and institutionalized religion, I strike out for some vinegar and salt of the city—not the dens of iniquity—but an exhibit at the National Gallery East Wing, a concert at the Kennedy Center, a play at the Kreeger. I find Jesus' night visit "over to the other side" affirming my own dash out, dash back.

Took Jesus along, just as he was. This phrase leaves everything to one's imagination speaks to me metaphorically. Don't make Jesus, the divine guest in your life's boat, into your own image. He rides just as he is. Not as a kind of Donald Trump or Bill Gates entrepreneurial capitalistic genius coveted by every poor religious organization or financially stressed middle-class Christian home. Not as a kind of Pat—Buchanan or Robertson—of neoconservative Republicanism courted by frightened fundamentalist baying for the Lord's prayer to be put back into public schools. Not the liberal grand marshalls of gay pride marches, nor apostle of hooks-and-eyes Amish, nor guerrilla leader of liberation theologs. Jesus wasn't an Anabaptist or Calvinist or Papal Nuncio! He rides just as he is—in his own image, not one convenient for our social strata or political quirk or economic bite.

Also other boats. Whose boats were commandeered, their owners awakening next morning to find them gone? Irritated with the wharf guard's remarks: "The master hath need of them—be glad he didn't also take your ass!" How many boats? How many men per boat? Who rowed? If three or four per boat, were Peter, James and John already intimate with Jesus? Did the others chaff at their exclusion from that forming inner circle? How smart was it to go out on the lake at night—with no moon, a portent of a possible storm? Again, metaphorically: so Jesus heads into the dark side of nature, straight into the social squall, taking us along.

Sleeping on a cushion. Did the cushion come with the boat or specially provided? By whom? What stuffing: goose down or corn shucks? Okay, Jesus was sleeping in a boat—at least he wasn't standing up, like George Washington "Crossing the Delaware!" Jesus, a presence, not a remover of difficult situations, provides the fearless peace of David's poem: "Even though I walk through the valley of the shadow of death, I will fear no evil, for you are with me. . . ."

Rebuked the wind and the waves. It's quite something for a modern mind to believe that God will adjust local weather to accommodate individual preference. At my university, lacking a large enough hall, we must conduct commencement exercises out-of-doors. April's fickle weather puts all of us, even the unbelievers, to prayer. ("April is in my mistress's face, but in her heart a cold December.") And that's what we often get, cold rain about 50/50—even with prayers by the resident evangelist, known for putting all heaven astir with his petitions.

"Who is this man?" Yes, the right question, even for today! Not: "Who am I?"—the wearisome query of twenty-first-century egos coddled by psycho-therapeutic-preachers. The question leads to soft repetition on every breath, the prayer of the publican: "Lord Jesus Christ, Son of God, have mercy on me." The Russian prayer: "Jesus, have mercy upon me." The shortest form of this prayer, "Kyrie eleison."

No Pigs in
the Peaceable Kingdom?
The Healing of a Demon-
Possessed Man

They crossed the lake to the region of the Gerasenes. A man with an evil spirit came out from the tombs where he lived. "Jesus," he howled, "swear to God you won't torture me! My name is Legion. Send us into the pigs." The evil spirit came out of the man and went into the two-thousand herd of pigs; they rushed down the hill and drowned in the lake. Their owners pled with Jesus to leave their region. Jesus sent the healed man home to his own family. —Mark 5: 1-20

HAVING CALMED THE WIND AND SEA from a squall, Jesus and his disciples arrived later that night on to the east shore region of the Gerasenes. While the narrative does not say, I want it to be night—for better theatrical staging of this eerie and frightening production. The full moon is again out after the sudden lake storm. And we all suspect that people—if not ourselves, surely our spouses and colleagues—are a little more mad at full moon than other nights.

Out from the tombs, limestone caves used for burial, rushes a demon-possessed man, naked, beard and hair matted with filth, dangling broken chains, scarred with dried blood. Oddly, he recognizes Jesus; his devils scream, not for deliverance, but preservation in a herd of pigs. The request is granted; they rush down a slope and drown in the lake.

"Howling in madness among the tombs." With every reading of this narrative, my heart wrenches for this poor fellow. I do not mean to be sentimental—but his is a madness not of his own making. His, while violent with torments, springs from the broken heart of an Ophelia, gently distributing her rosemary and pansies, fennel and columbines; and rue—that emblem of repentance—for others, for herself, that bitter herb of sorrow, that "herb of grace o' Sundays."

The mad fellow in the tombs did not cultivate a private lust for a public post, beseeching the prince of devils to empower him, as did Lady Macbeth:

. . . . Come, you spirits
That tend on mortal thoughts, unsex me here.
And fill me from the crown to the toe top-full
Of direst cruelty! make thick my blood;
Stop up the access and passage to remorse. . . .

Perhaps his howling was that of Randall Thompson's "Peaceable Kingdom" text from Isaiah: "Howl ye. . . ! Howl ye. . . !" (13:6). Once when I had a good tenor voice I twice howled with a choir this chorus. The howls of grief for sin that precedes the ushering in of the new kingdom, such as Edward Hicks, that preaching Quaker of Pennsylvania, paints in his oil by the same title. In the print in my wife's office, I search among Hick's animals for a restored mad man petting a pig—but find none. Maybe there is no room in the Peaceable Kingdom for pigs.

His name is "Legion," a word he borrows from the Roman occupiers, their term for a division of 6,000 soldiers. By urging the poor fellow to name his demons, Jesus uses a bit of Freudian (well, pre-Freudian!) psychology. When spoken aloud, the evil is broken. To convince him of his release, Jesus orders the legion of 6,000 devils to enter into 2,000 pigs. Three devils to a pig! Little wonder they rush to their drowning.

This is not a story for squeamish, sentimental animal rights people—such as the woman interviewed recently on the evening television news. She collected stray dogs; with therapy and anti-depressants-for-pet-pills, she restored them to health. Dogs matter too, I'll give her that. But had she heard of the wretched state of a million Bangladeshis, of the ten thousand abandoned street children of a half dozen South American city streets?

Granted, the pigs' owner was not consulted. Even had he been asked—"The Lord hath need of your 2,000 pigs. Okay?"—what would we say with him about this divine equation: the restoration of one man to sanity is worth the destruction of two thousand pigs? Is this too an example of the economy within the new kingdom of Jesus? Or is Jesus, a good Jew who is anti-pig—"You must not eat their meat or touch their carcasses; they are unclean" (Lev. 11:7)—simply reckless with Gentile property? Or is Jesus demonstrating that he does not accommodate himself to any culture? Are we instead seeing that, because he is Lord of all peoples, he judges all cultures?

The Muslim Somalis would cheer this story, for they too despise pigs. I know from an experience. At an interior school, alone, I was petitioned by village small-plot farmers to shoot the hippos which came out at nights and ravished their corn plots by the Shebelli River. Reluctantly agreeing, I plotted a bit of deceit: aim a bit high and only scare them away. In the thick, wet night, I stupidly aimed badly and shot one. It fell into their irrigation ditch.

In the morning when I used the mission truck to pull it away with a rope, no one would touch the dead hippo. The stream of villagers, arriving for the viewing, cleared their throats and spat on him. "It's a pig," they said, mouths full of disgust. So one old village infidel and I stepped into the muddy irrigation ditch to wrestle with roping my hippo. Cheers went up at our hauling "the pig" into the bush for the hyenas and vultures.

"Please leave our region!" the townsfolk pled. These members of Decapolis ("Ten Towns"), a Gentile city-state of pleasant temples, amphitheaters, and white plazas with marble gods and goddesses, didn't want their way of lives disturbed. Perhaps they too, like his disciples, said, "Who is this man?" Not with awe, but scorn: "Who does this fellow think he is—to come here and destroy our property?"

22

....

Jesus and Two Women
One Dead, One Sick

*One of the synagogue rulers, Jairus, came to Jesus. He fell at his feet
and pleaded earnestly. "My little daughter is dying. Come and put
your hands on her so that she will be healed." So Jesus went with him.
In the large crowd was a woman who had been subject to bleeding for
twelve years. She touched his cloak and was healed immediately.
—Mark 5:21-43*

A SYNAGOGUE PRESIDENT ORGANIZED WORSHIP and maintained
order during public services. Not a preacher, but as chairperson
of the church council, he was a pillar of respectability in the
town's religious life. Yet his daughter's feverish delirium drove
him from townhouse to lakeside, from Levitical priest to heretical teacher. There, finding Jesus, Jairus gladly threw aside his dignity, threw himself at Jesus' feet. "My little daughter is dying.
Come, put your hands on her so that she will be healed and live."

Jairus is not the first desperate aristocrat to step out of privilege for help. Syrian Prime Minister Naaman swallows national
and personal pride. As instructed by a mere servant of the Jewish
prophet Elisha, His Excellency steps into the muddy Jordan for a
washing away of his leprosy. Centuries later, the twenty-year-old
Alexander the Great, King of Macedonia, on a visit to newly
conquered Corinth expects to be greeted by that city's resident
philosopher Diogenes, founder of Cynicism. Alexander was no

slouch at philosophical studies, having the great Aristotle for a teacher. Yet, he needs this lesser philosopher's attention. Surely Diogenes, this God-born genius, will acknowledge the conqueror's power.

Not finding the philosopher among the Corinthian statesmen to welcome him, Alexander determines to call on Diogenes. But Diogenes says nothing, until after Alexander's query: "What can I do for you, philosopher?" Diogenes says, "Step aside; you're blocking the sunlight."

Jairus, and these other great men, learned to set aside prejudice, "being down on somebody you're not up on," as Gordon Allport writes a slangy definition for the term. Or, less slangy, here is Thomas Aquinas' definition of prejudice: "thinking ill of others without sufficient warrant." Desperation helps slay such attitudes.

Every parent with a critically sick child knows the twist of that knife in the gut. Not a few have prayed in tears, with hands on the burning deadly quiet child, for God to transfer the pain to themselves. My own act, my own prayer—but never answered. Yet none of my children died. Not even the son who dozed off and rolled his mother's car. He walked away from a totaled car with an inch scratch on his little finger. Yet his classmate, also a good lad, going home late from duties with a rescue squad, fell asleep, rammed a tree, and died. While I can fathom the terror of Jairus, I cannot imagine the grief of that boy's father called out at night to collect his young son, dead against a thick tree.

Suddenly I find that I am thinking of lines from Ben Jonsons' Epigram 45: "On My First Son," written on the occasion of the boy's death.

> Farewell, thou child of my right hand and joy!
> My sin was too much hope of thee, lov'd boy;
> Seven years thou wert lent to me, and I thee pay, . . .
> Rest in soft peace, and ask'd, say here doth lie
> Ben Jonson his best piece of poetry.
> For whose sake, henceforth, all his vows be such
> As what he loves may never like too much.

Elegant and conversational of tone, it's the poem's toughness that startles the reader. Not only a lament for a dead young son but also a confession that a father's love, a father's grief, can be a sin. Jonson prays that he will learn now to distinguish between loving and liking, that he will learn to love the Christ who gifts the Jonson household with a child as a loan, as a vehicle for grace in his life. Sin is to have placed hope for happiness solely in a son, a lent gift, and not in the Giver.

We do not know what illness seized Jairus' young daughter. But Jesus is right: she is not dead, she is asleep (in a coma). I like to think she is experiencing her first menses—in excruciating pain, she faints dead away. Thus blood links these two stories, as does the number 12: the daughter's age (5:42); the length of the woman's bloody illness (5:25). Also connecting the stories is the gesture of faith: Jairus and the sick woman "fell at Jesus' feet" (5:22; 5:33).

But first the unnamed woman touches Jesus. She has to know the Levitical law: "When a woman has a bloody discharge beyond her monthly period. . . anything she touches is unclean" (15:25-27). But she is desperate, and Mark gets in a sly dig at medics with the observation that "For twelve years she had suffered a great deal under the care of many doctors and had spent all she had, yet instead of getting better she grew worse" (5:26).

Wearing on her upper leg amulets filled with ashes of ostrich egg or kernels of corn from an ass's dung, drinking potions of dandelion wine or mare's milk—nothing cured her. So she touches Jesus, confers on him her own uncleanness. He carries her "filth" away, acknowledging, "Daughter, your faith has healed you."

And then he goes on to Jairus' dead daughter. "Have faith," he says to the bereaved father on their learning from servants the girl died. "*Talitha koum*!"—"Maiden, arise!" To her dad, Jesus says, "Give her something to eat." I believe Jairus threw a great feast. Clean and unclean ate together that day! A child was alive, again!

On Going Home
A Prophet Without Honor

Jesus went to his home town. . . to teach in the Synagogue. Many were amazed at his wisdom: "Isn't this the carpenter? Isn't this Mary's son? Aren't his brothers and sisters with us?" And they took offense at him. Jesus said, "A prophet is not without honor except in his hometown."
—Mark 6:1-6

"YOU CAN'T GO HOME AGAIN," THOMAS WOLFE, American southern writer, famously declares through the title of one of his novels. He could have been illustrating Jesus' attempts to teach in hometown Nazareth.

But other American voices in a Frost poem differ about homegoing. "Silas is back," the wife says, "be kind." She speaks of an old, broken hired man who has pitched up again. "He has come home to die," she adds. The husband mocks her gently with: "Home?—Home is the place where, when you have to go there, they have to take you in." The wife's rejoinder: "I should have called it something you somehow haven't to deserve." Here the attitude about homecoming is ambiguous, both piquant and sorrowful.

Perhaps no one better catches our American mixed feelings about homecoming than does popular illustrator Norman Rockwell. Nearly half of a random fifty of his paintings touch on home scenes, often so nostalgic as to risk sentimentality, a keen stab to the heart, a reminder of what is loss, gone forever for most people, urban and rural. Examples: his Thanksgiving table scene, the homecoming of a GI after war, the family outing.

One recent summer a Hagerstown, Maryland, niece resurrected the gathering of my extended Eby family after a lapse of nearly ten years. For years I'd wanted my wife and children, in-law children, and granddaughters to see the farm mansion of my birth and childhood, the quaint two-room school at Cearfoss, the severe Reiffs Mennonite Church, the graveyard where four generations of Ebys are buried, the three homes I lived in after moving from the farm. Now was the chance, on a Saturday afternoon before the Sunday gathering of the full tribe.

Visits to old home places are often both satisfying and upsetting. Attempts at modernization render a Victorian structure hideous; nothing remains of a mother's handsome traffic-stopping flower beds; a Pizza Hut sits in the cornfield of my youth—yet the old Norway maple in whose stout arms I dreamed away many a boyhood's summer afternoon still endures.

More painful was the family visit the next afternoon. I am a freak. I have wrought freaks—I and my wife and children are the only college graduates. We are the misfits, the only professionals among the farmers and small businessmen. Halfway through the twelve-minute speech I'd been honored to give, I was visited with remorse, visited too with pride: *These are your blood kin*, I thought, *but your measure is taken elsewhere, by people who matter much to you.* I drove home in a blue funk.

Unlike Jesus on his home visit, I experienced nothing—neither honor: "He is a college prof!" spoken by some niece with pride; nor dishonor: "He's only a teacher!" Except for an elder brother who pled with my parents to let me go to college, few of my people have blessed me in my career away from Nazareth. Except for an ultra-conservative nephew who fears my contamination of his children, none has bothered to scorn my teaching secular literature in a church synagogue.

I'd be happy, now in retirement, to be known as . . . "Isn't this the carpenter?" I am proud of my only begotten carpenter son. I admire the precision cuts of solid oak trim his strong hands sawed for the Strite house. I love to stroll through our local super Lowes and finger shiny tools, stroke fine veneer panel. I delight in visiting our local furniture gallery of handmade tables and chairs of solid walnut and mahogany.

So did Jesus' homefolks despise him because he was once a working man and no theologian with M.Div and Ph.D.? Did they mean to imply, "He's no better than us, why should he teach us?" Or is it only the old case: "Familiarity breeds contempt"?

When we are so close to the great men and women who would lead us, we often see only their "feet of clay" instead of their "head of gold, their chest and arms of silver, their belly and thighs of bronze, their legs of iron" (Dan. 2:33)? I embrace as truth, against the contemporary whom/what-can-I-blame syndrome, the epigrammatic rhyming couplet of Alexander Pope:

> Honor and shame from no condition arise.
> Act well your part, for there all the honor lies.

So, it's not that I am a carpenter, or a son of a farmer, or looked on a trash-filled street in my youth, or had poor potty training that matters. Nor is it worth a fig that I was born into a political dynasty or old money. Nor does my being a circumcised Hebrew, Pharisee. Like the apostle Paul, "all these I consider as rubbish" (though I much prefer the gristle of King James English—"all these I do count as dung" or "bullshit" in the parlance of my young students).

Rather, it's how well I use my tools: compass, plane, saw, hammer, chisel, in the making of a house, boat, oxen yoke, threshing tool, sluice gate, cart wheel, or coffin that matters. How I break open with clarity Mann's *Death in Venice*, peel away the hackneyed dead stalks of a student's prose, wrench from the muddle of my own mind a sentence that sings beauty and goodness and truth—there I am not without honor. In the end, I guess, for some, it little matters how the homefolk see us?

······················

Dressed for Witness
Jesus Sends out
the Twelve

Jesus sent out the twelve, two by two. "Take nothing but a staff—no bread, bag, or wallet. Wear sandals but not an extra tunic." If any village won't receive your message, shake the dust off your feet and leave." They went out; they preached; they healed. —Mark 6:7-13

SENT—WITHOUT A BAGEL, A CARPETBAG, or a single buck—not even a fresh pair of briefs. But be sure to take a sensible pair of walking shoes, Adidas or Nikes. Wear no religious costume to set you apart from the clothes of the common villagers. Embrace the contemporary style: faded blue jeans and a flannel shirt. No smart uniform to mark you as one of the special Galilean twelve. Nothing to warn people, "Pious man walking."

Such specific details about what to wear for witnessing got me wondering what the common Jewish man of Jesus' time wore. Not the fringed and tasseled ephod of the priestly set, not the silk socks and lederhosen of palace princes, nor the mail and leather of military guards. But the clothing of the green grocer, fisher, farmer. I consulted a short history of Palestinian clothing: *A tunic*: the precursor to underwear, a feedbag with holes for head and arms, not unlike the sacque—that Parisian frock of the 1960s, or the shirt-like night gown of Dickens' Scrooge.

A cloak: a robe, sheet, blanket; looped across the shoulders; worn by Jesus in every nursery Sunday school picture; usually blue, sometimes seamless.

A girdle: a five-inch leather belt, not unlike a cowboy's without the turquoise-studded buckle. When you hitched up your ankle-length tunic—to wash your mother-in-law's kitchen flags or shear sheep—you tucked the hem into the girdle.

A head dress: a square piece of cloth draped over the head; held in place by a head band, that precursor to the athletic sweat band.

Sandals: made of cow-hide leather, woven reed, or sandal wood—a precursor to the Dutch wooden shoe, the European clog. Travelers often carried sandals, putting them on as they entered a town: like Dewey Dell approaching Jefferson in Faulkner's *As I Lay Dying;* like my wife in her African childhood walking barefoot on dusty foot paths through the bush, her canvas shoes laced together and carried on her head; like her African playmates, stopping at the church door, brushing their feet, and putting on their shoes to enter the holy place.

What to wear is seldom addressed in holy Scripture. The wearing of gold offended St. Paul; women in slacks made a Levite look the other way; prophets railed against Babylonian silk, more for what it symbolized as garments of the economic oppressor than for its fleshy kiss of fabric to skin. But attitudes toward clothing are common—particularly in the New Testament. Remember Jesus' famous injunction: "Don't worry about . . . what you will wear! Look at the lilies!"

Yet all religious people hanker for clothing: a saffron robe for a Buddhist monk, a pleated wimple for a nun, a coarse-woven cowl with a coil of rope for a Capuchin father. And a plain high-collar, frock-tail coat for my ultra-conservative Mennonite men.

My tiny conference of socially backwater peoples has a preoccupation with what to wear. So fearful are they of conforming to the world, their teaching becomes an ironic inversion of their Lord's command: "Take no thought for what you should wear!" What to wear for witness mattered. Trudging along streets to distribute our religious tracts, or preach in the city prison, or sing at the poor house, we wore our plain clothes as witness of being set apart ("Be not conformed!") from common fellows who by their stylish clothes (even if they were out-of-style by two decades!) showed they lacked a proper application of their alleged Christian faith.

And years later, during the Vietnam War, carrying my pacifist convictions into the political arena, I marched with Philadelphia Quakers and picketed President Lyndon B. Johnson's White House. Although I now wore a tie and a civilian jacket, what one wore to witness apparently still mattered to some, as I learned during that two-hour morning vigil. We several hundred people stood at arms' length from each other outside the iron picket fence. On either side of me were young Quaker women. An elderly, neatly dressed gentleman passing by, read our sign imploring the American government to stop the bombing then stepped over to me. "You people are fools! Look at her"—he gestured to the lass beside me. "You haven't the sense to dress decently in public, putting yourselves on display—yet, you think you're smart enough to tell Johnson to stop a war."

I looked at the young woman beside me. She wore a miniskirt, as did my secretary back in the home office, so short it barely covered the droop of her pear-shaped bottom. She returned my gaze with a wry lift of her pert nose.

And one Easter, many years ago, finding ourselves in New York City, my wife and I lined up for the second service at Marble Collegiate Church. Norman Vincent Peale teased the ladies about their Easter hats of fruits, flowers, and feathers. "But we know: these, too, are an outward adornment of a new heart!" he pontificated. I looked at my wife's small black hat-like bonnet. So if we believe that hats make the woman, did "low in the grave she still lay"? We silly Christians fret about our clothes—about what is proper for witness, despite our Lord's freeing dismissal!

God's Elect, God's Neglect? John the Baptist Beheaded

Herod himself ordered John the Baptist's arrest, for saying his marriage to Herodias was unlawful. She wanted to kill John, but Herod protected him, knowing him to be righteous. On Herod's birthday, Herodias' daughter Salome danced so well Herod offered her anything she wanted. Consulting her mother, she said: "I'll have the head of John the Baptist on a platter." Greatly distressed, Herod kept his word.
—Mark 6:14-29

FEW STORIES IN THE NEW TESTAMENT put me in so great a blue funk as does God's neglect of his elect—John the Baptist. Reading the story again last night, sleeping on it, writing on it this morning, I shall be brooding on it for days.

John comes out of the fiery desert with a fiery message of repentance. He is the last harbinger of the Messiah. He understands the importance of his message, understands, too, his insignificance as messenger. He baptizes his cousin, Jesus, into a public ministry. He dares to twist the regal nose of the political aristocracy, to tell Herod, King of Galilee province, that his second marriage is not only shameful but a sin according to Levitical law. Herodias is the daughter of his half-brother Aristobulus;

therefore Herod married his niece. Herodias is also the divorced wife of his half-brother Philip; thus Herod married his sister-in-law. So she gets her knickers in a knot over being called Sin. The Baptist goes directly to jail.

His prison is on the Dead Seas's east shore. From his cave cell he stares at his lovely desert. This wild free spirit, son of wilderness, cannot roam there. No wonder he sinks into a depression from which doubts arise. "Jesus, are you the One? Or. . . ?"

To his own disciples, Jesus gives a ringing endorsement: "I tell you the truth: Among those born of women there has not risen anyone greater than John the Baptist."

On his own birthday Herod throws an all-night party. I imagine in the manner of the movie version of Jay Gatsby's summer weekend drunken bashes at his Long Island home—vast, cultured vulgarity. Salome, another Daisy Buchanan, dances before the drunken guests, a role not for royalty, but for hired professional prostitutes, the Greco-Roman call girls. And the dance is a licentious pantomime of promiscuous sex. The old goat, lusting for his step-daughter, loses his head and offers her anything she wants. "John the Baptist's head on a silver platter!" whispers Herodias. The king trapped, the queen gets her revenge.

It's high theatrical tragedy. No wonder artists turn to it for a short story, a drama, an opera, as Strauss' "Dance of the Seven Veils" in his "Salome." I remember her dance in that production as all nudity, silk scarves, and wild loose hair. But I want more than high theater. I want more than Jesus' ringing endorsement. I want justice for John, intervention from God, not neglect of his imprisoned prophet. I want assurance.

Assurance? Do I want to entrust myself to this God? Recommend his providence to my children? This God who could not—or would not—care for this forerunner to his Son? I know such questions seem not just heretical but profane.

Such are the questions that caused an intimate friend of mine to write, "While faith is the center of your being, that center has forever been unstable and problematic. Your faith has made you strong and it has made you weak. All of your teaching, all that you read, all that you write is a reflection of this di-chotomy, and you understand with something like despair that it will remain like this until the end. . . . [You] look around for someone to knock on the fool head. You believe that since God created this situation, he ought to help out. But he will not al-ways, you've discovered, help out. Indeed, he has walked out."

When I remember, I find myself in fine company with Jere-miah's complaints against divine management: "You are always righteous, O Lord, when I bring a case before you. Yet, I would speak with you about *your justice*: Why does the way of the wicked prosper? Why do all the faithless live at ease?" (12:1-3, italics mine). Yet I also recall Jeremiah's praise: "Blessed is the man who trusts in the Lord. He will be like a tree planted by the water" (17:7,8).

But J. B.'s tree was cut down, its leaves still green. Did it ever bear fruit? Gerard Manley Hopkins knew keenly this divine ne-glect. In one Dublin sonnet of desolation he writes of looking on village sots and greening nature. Then:

> . . . birds build—but not I build; no, but strain,
> Times's eunuch, and not breed one work that wakes.
> Mine, O thou lord of life, send my roots rain.

Reading in Annie Dillard's *For the Time Being* only aids my grief. So bleak is her assembly of fact and anecdote concerning the wastage of humans as to make nature downright profligate. Hers is a more eclectic garnering of ideas and reflections on Reynolds Price's themes in *To a Man in the Fire*—is there a God and does he care?

A British journalist, observing Mother Theresa in Calcutta, puts the hard truth in this manner: "Either life is always and in all circumstances sacred, or intrinsically of no account; it is in-conceivable that it should be in some cases the one, and in some the other" (Dillard, 160). John's star, fiery in the night, burned out quickly. Imprisoned, neglected, beheaded. We are left with a puzzle: Some humans are of no account? Some sacred? Because we know not who is which, we should treat all as in God's image?

Bread and Fish
Jesus Feeds the Five Thousand

The Twelve returned from their teaching mission. Jesus said: "Come to a quiet place and rest." But Jesus saw the crowd and had compassion. "Give them something to eat," he said. "There are five loaves and two fish," they reported. So the crowd sat down on the green grass and ate until satisfied. The disciples picked up twelve basketfuls of broken bread and fish. The number of men was five thousand.
—Mark 6:30-44

JESUS' FEEDING OF THE FIVE THOUSAND stunned his disciples. All four of the gospelers wrote it up—in fact, it's the only miracle related by all four! Thus it's not easy to explain away this extraordinary incident, although many Christians who don't want a transcendent Christ strain for a rational explanation: the crowd of men (plus a thousand women, two thousand children?) seeing a boy peel some bread and fish out of the folds of his belted tunic felt guilty, felt moved to share at Jesus' prayer of consecration, brought out their own foodstuffs. Or the story is a foreshadowing symbol, a physical manifestation of the Eucharist to come. But I want a miracle, even at the risk of Jesus' rebuke: you wicked and unbelieving generation ask for a miraculous sign to undergird your faith.

The twelve had been so pressed on their first preaching and healing mission they reported to Jesus: "We didn't even have a chance to eat!" Jesus understood the limits of flesh. He was, after all, incarnate now—man in the flesh. So his response was compassionate: "Come with me by yourselves to a quiet place and get some rest." With that, they got back into the boat and set out for the other shore.

But the wind had dropped; the exhausted disciples could not row fast. The crowds ran around the north end of the lake and beat the slow boat. "A large crowd gathered." The disciples' attempt at retreat failed, their need for privacy invaded. But Jesus did not disappoint the crowd, did not query their motives—even, surely, as some were sizing him up as their next Maccabean guerrilla leader to fight for Palestinian freedom.

"This is a remote place, and it's already very late. Send the people away so they can go to the villages and buy themselves something to eat." The hungry disciples had food on their minds. Their suggestion of what to do with five thousand hungry Jewish men, plus another couple thousand women and children, was sane. It would take an eight month's salary to feed them—or a miracle. So, Jesus' rejoinder, "You feed them," was met with questions of disbelief.

Indeed it might seem the time for a miracle. "Tell these stones to become bread." The suggestion seems miraculous enough. Jesus had resisted that earlier sly suggestion by the Devil in the wilderness; himself hungry then, he did not want to use his power for self-indulgence. But this scene was surely different. On command Jesus could turn Palestinian pebbles into pumpernickel (well, maybe not pumpernickel; its Germanic derivatives hint at its reputed indigestibility: pumper = flatulence; nickel = devilish goblin) but surely rye bagels, sourdough biscuits, or hot cross buns. Or maybe manna.

"What is it? Manna? Manna?" the excited hungry nomadic Jewish tribe cried that first morning a strange substance, "thin flakes like frost, appeared on the desert floor" (Exod. 16:14). "It was white like coriander seed and tasted like wafers made with honey" (16:31). Later Jesus called it "bread of heaven." Still later, disbelieving European scientists declared the substance to be the excretion of some insect feeding on tamarisk trees! No matter; it was good stuff—one wanted to get this recipe from God. God's Son could surely serve it up again.

But he didn't. Instead, he said to the hungry twelve, dead tired on their feet: "Give them [all eight thousand?] something to eat." And this was only the first of other mass feedings with real bread the disciples were made to join Jesus in serving. Later there would be a group of four thousand men. Still later, there would be an early morning lakeside breakfast of fish and bread when after his resurrection Jesus would again eat with most of his disciples. And reinstate Peter, still sorrowful for his denial of Jesus at the arraignment leading to his execution. To him, Jesus would say, "Feed my lambs. Take care of my sheep. Feed my sheep." Jesus passed on to his disciples the commission of compassion then, just as now he looked on the five thousand like "sheep without a shepherd."

There were fish, too. Little sun-dried salt fish—not fresh ones, which, like visitors, stink in three days. They were real fish—a small boy's belted snack—which, together with the bread, nourished thousands that day. But the fish later also became a sacred symbol for the early Christians hiding from the persecution by stupid Romans. The Greek word for fish, *ichthus,* has five component letters to make a sacred acrostic for the initials of the five Greek words that mean "Jesus Christ, Son of God, Savior." My Christ is not only bread; my Christ is also fish.

The small necessities of life—barley loaves and dried fish—offered to Christ can become that quantum leap of nourishment for others beyond oneself, beyond one's own honest hunger. "Give us this day, our daily bread" that we might "feed the lambs, feed the sheep." And "if our enemy is hungry, give him food to eat," too.

Bread and Waves
Jesus Walks on the Water

Immediately Jesus made his disciples go back to Bethsaida by boat.
Then he dismissed the crowd and went up on a mountain to pray.
Later, he saw the disciples straining at the oars. About the fourth watch
he went to them, walking on the lake. Terrified, they cried out. Imme-
diately he said, "It is I." He climbed into the boat and the wind died
down. —Mark 6:45-56

"IMMEDIATELY" (THE FIRST OF TWO immediatelys in this passage)
Jesus dismissed his disciples. "Get in the boat, go back across the
lake to Bethsaida." Why this sudden instruction to the weary
twelve? Gospeler John gives the clue. After the feeding of the five
thousand, the people began to say, "Surely this is the prophet
who . . . ." Jesus "knew they intended to make him king by force"
(6:15). This restless, demanding mob wanted not only bread but
a circus. Again they were remembering the national political and
religious heroes of their great-grandparents, the Maccabees.

That powerful dynasty successfully fought off Syrian attempts to impose Hellenistic culture on the Jews. As if you could
convert a Jew by defiling his temple at Jerusalem by sacrificing
swine to Zeus over the high altar for burnt offerings to Jehovah!
Using guerrilla tactics from their mountain hide-outs, they de-
feated the Syrian military contingent. For the next 103 years, the
Jews relished political and religious freedom. Then came the Ro-

mans. Those Jews who had not accommodated themselves to the imperial power were ready to seize on another Judas Maccabaeus.

But the politics of Jesus was one of yeast, the quiet work of leaven in a bowl of dough. He did not want a mob howling in protest at Herod's Winter Palace in St. Pete. He would use the seduction of pacifism, not the force of fascism. He would not endorse the violence of a liberation theology. He was not the Christ of a Christian Coalition or People for the American Way, giving themselves to building God's kingdom on earth.

This story is all about weather, too. The wind the disciples needed in the afternoon, stalled on the lake, now had arisen at nightfall and blew stiff out of the northwest. If they left shortly after sundown, they were still "straining at the oars" nearly nine hours later. My biblical atlas shows that at this section of the lake it is only four or five miles across, from side to side. John says, "They had rowed three or three and a half miles" (6:19). The wind had blown in a clear sky; the moon was out. Jesus from his mountain top "saw the disciples. . . in the middle of the lake."

"About the fourth watch of the night he went out to them." Now the Mediterranean time-keeping was based on sun-rise to sun-set. The night had four watches: 6:00 p.m. to 9:00 p.m.; 9:00 p.m. to 12:00 midnight; midnight to 3:00 a.m.; 3:00 a.m. to 6:00 sunrise.

It is possible to read in a time-lapse between Jesus' first sighting the disciples straining at the oars and his going to them sometime after three in the morning. I don't think he went as soon as he saw them in trouble. Did he want them to feel helpless for six to eight hours before a fickle night wind over the lake? His compassion was not the softness of suburbia. Rather, the disciples learned strength through struggle. That night on the lake was metaphor, or T. S. Eliot's "objective correlative," for the soul's struggles against spiritual forces in high places.

At last Jesus arrived, "having taken his good old time," walking on the water. Then, this troubling phrase: "He was about to pass by them." What's this cat-and-mouse game all about? Had-n't the chaps, deprived of good food and rest and now battling a boat-stalling wind, suffered enough? One more test—about what?

In the strange silvery moonlight, his form, ghostlike, frightened the men. Terrified, might they think it to be the head or a hump of the Loch Ness monster of Lake Galilee? Their terror takes me to Coleridge's poor blokes in "The Rime of the Ancient Mariner." Stymied by the loss of a southern wind for their sails, they languish under a copper sun.

> Day after day, day after day,
> We stuck, nor breath nor motion;
> As idle as a painted ship
> Upon a painted ocean.

A specter-ship rides to them without wind or tide. Ghostly Death and Death-in-Life dice for the ship's crew. They all die—save one, the Ancient Mariner, like Melville's Ishmael, like Job's messenger: "And I only am escaped alone to tell thee" (1:14-19).

Terrified, the disciples cry out. And here's the second "immediately": He said, "It is I." The disciples, experiencing a physical "dark night of the soul," distracted by fear's distortion, did not recognize their Teacher. The paradox: what they thought would harm was the one come to save. Like the narrator in Thompson's "The Hound of Heaven," "Is my gloom, after all, / Shade of His hand, outstretched caressingly?" What the exhausted narrator under shadow felt to be a hand raised to smite was the Hand of Grace raised to restore. Similarly, the disciples: Through the distortion of their exhaustion and terror, they were tested. Could they acknowledge correctly the presence of their Teacher?

Then Jesus stepped into the maelstrom of his disciples' lives and all was calmed. Yet I am left thinking that he who steps into our fragile boat and calms a storm is also he who steps into our lethargic lives and churns up a storm.

Pork and Pomegranates
Unclean and Clean

The Pharisees saw Jesus' disciples eating with unwashed hands. "Jesus, why don't your men live according to the traditions of the elders?" Jesus spoke to the crowd, "Listen, nothing that enters a person from the outside can make him unclean." (In saying this, Jesus declared all foods clean.) "What comes out of a person is what makes him unclean." —Mark 7: 1-23

A GOOD JEW WASHED WHEN HE CAME FROM the market and before he handled food—not just for sanitary reasons. Gentiles were unclean, as were women in their period, and pigs, so the Jewish lawyers codifying Jehovah's broad principles about cleanliness had established hundreds of laws concerning ceremonial washing. Jesus dismissed those "traditions of the elders," declaring "their teachings are but rules taught by men."

It is all absolutely breathtaking: With a few sentences spoken one afternoon in Galilee, Jesus wiped out laws, customs, traditions, taboos concerning his heritage's dietary and culinary centuries-old practices! The animals, too, of Leviticus 11—swine, camel, rabbit, vultures, owls, rats, lizards? Later, a similar revelation came to Peter praying on a housetop at noon. A sheet let down from heaven contained four-footed beasts, reptiles, and birds. The Voice said, "Do not call anything impure that God has made clean. Rise and eat" (Acts 10:15).

While food was often scarce in Palestine, the region had plenteous varieties of foodstuffs: beans, lentils, cucumbers, squash, figs, olives, pomegranates, breads, kid and venison meats, milk, cheese, quail, partridge, fish, butter, mulberries, melons, onions, leeks, garlic, dates, honey, nuts, raisins, fancy cakes, wines, and on and on. So Jesus, with his "all foods are clean"—was hardly preparing a wider selection of edibles on the smorgasbord for the hungry. Rather, he demonstrated how wide the gap between true and false religion. Defilement came from the gross imaginations of the heart, not what passed down the gullet. Cleanliness came from the washing by the water of his word, not from abstaining from a slice of hickory-smoked ham at Easter.

While "all foods are clean," and "all things are lawful, not all things are expedient"—gastronomically, nor gourmet-wise—"But thank you very much, Jesus!"

I loathe stewed cow tongue, okra, and oysters. Granted, some of the loathing results from the power of the imagination being greater than the power of the salivating glands. I cannot *not* think of the nose holes the cow's tongue has been up—a lingering memory from an observation of my impressionable farm-boy years. But some loathing rises from the appearance and feel of the food in the mouth: the oyster is not a peeled de-tailed mouse, the grit of the oyster might be a baby pearl-in-the-making. Stewed okra, slimy, slippery, can only be compared to the feel of mucus from a severe winter cold.

My early adults years in Somalia and Tanzania released me from the bland food of my Pennsylvania Dutch peasant heritage: lima beans, corn, mashed potatoes, roast beef, tapioca. All good hearty stuff, I suppose, but without sauces, creams, dressings, spices to kick it into something more lively. Yet much of the food in Africa is rightly oriented to peasantry, as compared to Asia. One need not get defensive about noting that. A simple check in my home town: how many African restaurants are there compared to Asian and Mediterranean? So, I did not learn to savor smoked camel milk in Somalia, while their cardamum-flavored tea surpasses the best British Earl Grey. Nor did I care for goat testicles and flying ants (termites) of Tanzania. Yet their coastal mango rivals any Georgia peach.

But one must allow for those foods which are soulful and nostalgic for particular peoples. I remember the breakfast grits at Ole Miss, the chitlins at Howard University, the boiled cabbages in London. And the ugali and tomato soup for my wife. Born and reared in Tanzania, daughter of pioneer missionaries, she often ate ugali—a stiff multi-grain mush—in the African village homes with her parents. And the tomato soup of her mother— not a cream of tomato, but a milky soup in which slices of stewed tomatoes float. These she served our children during my absences from dinner. Now that she is a grandmother and misses her deceased mother and the fled years of her simple African childhood, she restores her soul with Sunday evening tomato soup. I look on, clean of envy.

"Jesus declared all foods clean." Yes, but that was before processed foods, deep fried salty snacks, and the fast food fare of a dozen chains. Before airplanes, which allow for the packaging and shipping of plastic strawberries and tomatoes from California to northeastern cities in January. Before heart attacks, which—if you survive—ban chocolates, cheese, creams, colas. Before the endless studies which declare one year red beef to be bad, the next year, the innocent egg to be subterfuge.

What would my grandmothers with their rural gardens make of the food on my table: kiwi, fugi apples, lox and bagels, curried mussels, dal, sushi? Or of the ethnic restaurants in my small town: Thai, Nepalese, Indian, Chinese, Japanese, Greek, Mexican, Italian, Ethiopian? Perhaps all these foods prefigure that great heavenly banquet at which some from every nation and tribe shall sit down and eat a great feast, eat ambrosia with Christ. Until then, still one "hungers after righteousness" and for Him who is "the Bread of Life."

Children's Crumbs
The Faith of a Syrophoenician Woman

Jesus went to the vicinity of Tyre. He wanted to keep his presence secret. But as soon as a Greek woman, born in Syrian Phoenicia, heard about him, she fell at his feet and begged him to heal her demon-possessed daughter. He said, "It's not right to toss the children's bread to dogs." She replied, "Yes, Lord, but even the dogs under the table eat the children's crumbs." Jesus said, "Woman, for such a reply your daughter is healed." —Mark 7:24-30

HAVING WIPED OUT THE DISTINCTIONS between clean and unclean food, Jesus goes forty miles north to Tyre, a town in a Gentile country, as if to wipe out the distinctions between clean and unclean people. Tyre: an important seaport on the Mediterranean for ancient Phoenicia (today Southern Lebanon); a sturdy people, their sailors star-gazing until they were "the first to ever burst" into the wider seas, sailing at night by stars; their hand-blown glass, a cherished collectible.

The Jews by Jesus' time had garnered numerous experiences with the residents of Tyre. The earliest was during the land allotments on their arrival into Canaan with Joshua and Caleb. The bickering and leek-yearning first generation along with Moses were dead; the second generation of wilderness wanderers could now enter the Promised Land. Old Tyre, a Phoenician coastal town, was one of twenty-two towns named in the territory assigned to Asher and his clan (Josh. 19:28, 29). Probably neither Asher nor his great-grandchildren ever attempted to seize Tyre from those first rugged residents.

Later, King Solomon, a friend of King Hiram of Tyre, sent Hebrew boys to help cut timbers for his temple. "You know that we have no one who can fell cedars of Lebanon like you fellows," Solomon said with savvy wisdom. Still later, another Israeli king would traffic with Tyrenese. Ahab married Jezebel, daughter of a kingly family of old Phoenicia. As part of her royal trousseau came the priests of Baal. Her cultic worship with its sexual orgies of temple gods and goddesses became for years a fat hideous leech sucking at the spiritual life of Israel. Until Elijah, the Tishbite declared to King Ahab, "Dogs will devour Jezebel, that bitch, by the wall of Jezreel" (2 Kings 9:10). That word of the Lord by his prophet came true later when three eunuchs threw the painted queen from an open window to the stone-paved street (9:30-37).

So into that country, into Phoenicia, Jesus slips. Phoenicia, Syria, Egypt, Greece, Rome—simply naming Israel's neighbors reminds one of the advanced, sophisticated cultures which lay just outside Hebrew Palestine with its pastoral valleys of sheep and shepherds and small towns of common tradesmen. Why Jesus went there we can surmise. Herod was finding him, the embodiment of John the Baptist, to be a nuisance; the Pharisees and other leaders of orthodoxy found his blasphemous teachings made him worthy of death; Galilean mobs thought of liberation from Roman. Nowhere at home could he drop his identity and rest. Like a Billy Graham or a Roman Pope—recognizable anywhere in the world, they would have to travel incognito. Imagine the Pope without his satin skull cap, the evangelist behind designer shades and a Beatles' wig.

Then the clever exchange between Jesus and the desperate Gentile woman. Jesus pitched out a metaphor about children and dogs—perhaps the word was *bitch*—a term as offensive now as derogatory then. A smart woman, even though she lay prostrate at Jesus' feet, she rose to his bait, parried his reply with her own bit of wit. Desperate about her demon-possessed daughter, in tete-a-tete with this new preacher Jesus, she had nothing to lose with her risk of being cheeky. "Even dogs may eat the children's crumbs."

Even if Greek scholars are correct and Jesus perhaps used a term for dog that meant not a street cur but a lady's lap pet, we know Jews often referred to Gentiles as dogs. Even Jesus himself in his Sermon on the Mount said, "Do not give dogs what is sacred; do not throw pearls to pigs." Perhaps it was all in the tone of his pronouncements to the Syrophoenician woman. While we cannot hear the tone, we do know that he did not reject her. "Woman, for such a reply. . . !"—Jesus healed her daughter. The harshness of his words declaimed a statement of his priorities, on whom he would concentrate, of whom he'd make salt to preserve Israel's neighbors. Here in this Gentile town was a foretelling of the Acts of the apostle and the Holy Spirit: whom the Jews rejected, the Gentiles gained.

My own daughter as a young adult lay ill with a pseudo-tumor in the skull. The pressure there was off the doctor's gauge; the tappings of the spine, a searing pain. I would have in those days gladly embraced any divine insult—call me cur, call me sow—if I knew God would cure her.

And having written "cur," my mind (for something lighter?) flashed to Browning's poetic retort to Edward FitzGerald, on reading in that man's posthumously published letters his slight of Mrs. Browning: "Her death is rather a relief to me . . . no more poems [from her], thank God!" To which Mr. Browning in a white heat wrote his own rejoinder, a few lines of which follow:

> Aye, (she) dead! and were yourself alive, good Fitz,
> How to return you thanks would task my wits.
> Kicking you seems the common lot of curs—
> While more appropriate greeting lends you grace,
> Surely to spit there glorifies your face—
> Spitting from lips once sanctified by hers.

A Fine Fellow
The Healing of a Deaf
and Mute Man

Jesus went on to Sidon, down to Galilee and into Decapolis. People
brought him a deaf and mute man. Jesus took the man aside, away
from the crowd. He put his fingers in the man's ears and touched his
tongue with spit. With a deep sigh, Jesus said, "Be Opened!" Immedi-
ately he could hear and speak. The people were amazed. "He has done
everything well," they said of Jesus. —Mark 7:31-37

FROM TYRE NORTH TO SIDON, THEN SOUTH to Galilee, then east to
the region of Decapolis (Ten Towns)—Jesus and his twelve on a
walking tour, six to eight months long, some scholars guess.
Thirteen men together: the long days for walking, talking; the
long evenings for eating, sleeping. Alone, sober, without distraction, without illusions. The simple rites of sharing bread, sharing
bed, link these characters to the immemorial past and the eternal
present of all human activities.

The disciples learned to regard each other with affection—
different as they were, ex-fishers, ex-tax collector, ex-guerrilla
scout. They learned to view each other as a common species, and
knew they had nothing to fear from each other so long as they
shared in the essential human acts of eating, sleeping, and disci-
pling by their spiritual Teacher. They needed to learn that these
months of growing camaraderie would be essential to their post-

Ascension mission. They did not know at the time what we later readers of their story know with pathos—how fleeting was their bonding, how soon their Teacher's death would tear them apart, send them spiraling downward into spiritual depression. But for now, we envy them these months apart with their Teacher Jesus.

Into this small Society of Jesus some supporters brought their deaf-mute friend for healing. Nearly a repeat performance of the incident of the four chaps, who had earlier torn off a roof to let their paralytic friend down to Jesus on a healing mission (2:1-12). Here too no mention is made of the deaf-mute's faith. We are surprised, again, to discover that because of *their* faith, Jesus healed their friend. Again we're nudged into acknowledging that our own trust in God just might make it possible some day for a friend, a nephew, or others, to receive divine help. So holy is that notion—that I am a potential channel for God's grace to others—I hardly have breath to claim it.

The details of this little episode again distract and entertain the imaginations. "Jesus took the man aside, away from the crowd." For two reasons, I'm guessing. Neither Jesus nor his disciples needed just then a public spectacle of his power. And Jesus wanted to give the poor deaf-mute a bit of privacy, "far from the madding crowd." Poignant, tender pathos.

Another detail: Jesus spoke "with a deep sigh." Sometimes we sigh from weariness; sometimes we sigh with relief. Jesus might have sighed from exhaustion—we cannot know what spiritual and psychosomatic energies he tapped for healing physical deformities, for exorcism of evil spirits. Or might Jesus have sighed with relief, with a quiet resignation—even with happiness to be back into his routines after a lengthy leave? Quite possibly he had not cured anyone for eight months, not since the Syrophoenician woman back in Tyre. The sigh said it was good again to be about his Father's business.

And the last pleasant detail is Jesus' pantomime and touch. No wonder he chose privacy from the crowds, even if the twelve were witnesses. It would be quite something to have Jesus stick his fingers in your ears, to have his spit touch your tongue! An intimate treatment full of risk! Yet those who submit to the unconventional touch of the Lord find it restorative.

"He [Jesus] has done everything well," the crowd said, when they heard the deaf-mute answering their question about what all happened to him. A marvelous accolade! The crowd spoke a truth they did not fully understand. Their utterance hinted at the Perfect Man-Perfect God who brings shalom, whose kingdom is Eden restored, a Paradise regained. Even as Milton in his opening lines to his dramatic epic writes,

> I who erewhile the happy Garden sung,
> By one man's disobedience lost, now sing
> Recover'd Paradise to all mankind,
> By one man's firm obedience fully tried
> Through all temptation, and the Tempter foil'd
> In all his wiles, defeated and repuls't,
> And *Eden* rais'd in the waste Wilderness.

"He has done everything well." An epitaph I might crave for my tomb stone. Still full of gracelessness, I am no candidate to own that salute to Jesus. Nor am I like the elderly Benedictine monk friends of Kathleen Norris, of whom she writes in *Amazing Grace*: "They have a kind of polish, a gentle manner that has come from having been hard-scrubbed in the rough and tumble of communal living."

"He has a kind of polish, a gentle manner" was not said of me on retirement at the obligatory dinner, nor hardly will be two decades later, found at Oak Lea retirement community by my former fans of Faulkner. Other descriptors—honest and unsentimental words—come to mind, during this morning's moment of "centering." Words like: dour, crotchety, testy, blunt, impatient, irreverent, irritable, irascible. I am sure my colleagues who attempted over the years to give me a "hard scrubbing" have additional words. Some possibly not uttered in the polite society of a Christian academy. Too late, too tired, to do much renovation of character now. Yet, not outside a hard drubbing by Christ— but toward what end, I cannot imagine!

An Epiphanic Moment
Jesus Feeds the Four Thousand

The large crowds had nothing to eat for three days. "I have compassion on these people," Jesus said to his disciples. "We have nothing but seven loaves and a few small fish," they said. Jesus told the crowd to sit down; he blessed the food, the people ate and were satisfied. Then they got into a boat and went to Dalmanutha. Pharisees came and said, "Show us a sign." Jesus sighed and got back into the boat and crossed the lake to the other side. —Mark 8:1-13

I KNOW I SHOULD BE THINKING HARD: about this miracle of feeding four thousand people with seven loaves and a few fish, about this epiphanic moment not unlike that first Epiphany to the three old wise men, that first manifestation, first proclamation of the good news to the Gentiles, and here again to these Gentiles east of the lake; about hungry people, the hunger-gaunt people and vacant-eyed children of Kosovo, of southern Sudan, and a dozen other spots displaying "man's inhumanity to man"; about the strange topography of the region of Dalmanutha, where two thousand years later the skull of Neanderthal man will be found; about Jesus and the twelve rowing from one side of the lake to the other to escape crowds, then from that side back to the other to escape inquisition; about Jesus sighing, again, with hints of the inevitability of compassion fatigue—but. . . .

Just now I am looking out the window of my little office onto a lawn sprinkled with the golden coins of fallen birch leaves; and up into the October orange flare of maples; and beyond, up into the open skies above the meadow where the flickering wings of a thousand grackles fracture autumnal light; and still beyond, to the orchard of golden delicious apples, each tree still globed with bright gold fruit among the rust-flecked leaves—looking out on all that and thinking about the Pharisees clamoring, "Give us a sign from heaven."

The fools! All around them lay signs from heaven—not just this miracle-working Son of man destined to be Heaven's eternal resident Son. Look around! All living and growing and inanimate objects of nature give glory to God by their being exactly what he has destined them to be. This is the "inscape" of which poet Gerard Manley Hopkins writes, this inarticulate utterance by a natural object of an identity which it has from and in God; this inexhaustible spiritual sheen which radiates out through the fragile film of matter. This paradox: He who is spiritual manifests himself in the material, the physical, an only Son, and one God-loved world.

Jesus could have startled the staid Pharisees by singing out to them:

This is my Father's world; I rest me in the thought
Of rocks and trees, of skies and seas; His hand the wonders
    wrought.
The morning light, the lily white; He shines in all that's fair;
In the rustling grass I hear Him pass, He speaks to me every
    where.

But if that one-hundred-year-old melody by Maltbie Babcock seemed too icky-sweet for his temperament, for his critics' taste, Jesus could have given them some Henry van Dyke and Ludwig van Beethoven:

All thy works with joy surround thee,
earth and heav'n reflect thy rays,
stars and angels sing around thee,

center of unbroken praise. Field and forest,
vale and mountain,
blooming meadow, flashing sea,
chanting bird and flowing fountain,
call us to rejoice in thee.

Or raised his arms and "all the trees of the fields" would break out in a ferocious recitative of cellos and basses that opens that soaring choral fourth movement of Beethoven's Ninth. Even a few translated lines from Schiller's ode, a rather silly romantic gush about wanting to embrace "O ye millions and kiss the whole world of brothers," does not distract from the ecstasy of the earth's beauty:

All creation drinks joy from the breasts of nature;
all the good and all the bad follows in her rosy path.

(I don't much care for "rosy" here, but this is what one gets from a poet who sits with his feet in a lake on a balmy evening and vaporizes under a full moon.)

"A tree gives glory to God by being a tree," Thomas Merton declares in *New Seeds of Contemplation*. "It is expressing an idea (a sign, you thick-headed, weak-eyed scholarly Pharisees!) which is in God and which is not distinct from the essence of God, and therefore a tree imitates God by being a tree" (29). And I say,

The ocean praises God with its majestic restlessness.
The piedmont praises God with its wooded, rounded,
    green slopes.
The sun-blanched savannah praises God with its horizons,
    its grasses afire in the scintillating heat.
The leaf praises God with its fret of veins and serrated edges.

Like David's poem sent to the temple director of music to be scored into a motet:

The heavens declare the glory of God;
the skies proclaim the work of his hands.
Day after day they pour forth speech;
night after night they display knowledge.

Like Pierre Teilhard de Chardin, that Jesuit paleontologist, in his *Hymn to the Universe*: "Like those translucent materials which can be wholly illumined by a light enclosed within them, the world manifests itself to the Christian mystic as bathed in an inward light which brings out its structure, its relief, its depths. . . . It is the tranquil, mighty radiance born of the synthesis, in Jesus, of all the elements of the world" (88).

There are your signs from heaven, you Pharisees. If you have no eyes for these, why should Jesus waste on you another divine light-and-sound show?

More About Bread
The Yeast of the Pharisees and Herod

The disciples had forgotten to bring bread, except for one loaf they had with them in the boat. "Be careful," Jesus warned them. "Watch out for the yeast of the Pharisees and that of Herod." The disciples discussed this among themselves: "It's because we have no bread." Aware of their discussion, Jesus asked them: "Why are you still talking about having no bread? Do you still not understand." —Mark 8:14-21

HOW COULD ALL TWELVE HAVE FORGOTTEN to bring bread! They'd just "picked up seven basketfuls of broken pieces that were left over" (8:8). "O men! Don't leave planning for sandwiches to men!" Martha, sister of Mary, would have groaned. So who's to blame? If Judas kept the purse; if James, John, Simon Peter, and Andrew, the muscular quartet of fishermen, surely rowed the boat; it hardly ould have been lily-hand Levi, a banker–then how about Simon Zealot, a strategist? I'd make him responsible.

They did not have to pray, "Give us this day our daily bread"—they had it! One day-old loaf with them in the boat. One sort of lumpish-shaped thing the size of a wilderness rock— for the thirteen of them! No wonder the twelve talked bread among themselves. They'd just left seven basketfuls of good crusty bread-ends on the wharf. Bread their Teacher had given them. They could not bother their Teacher now for another bread miracle. They'd have to await the bread of Elijah's ravens. Bread as gift. "I am the Bread of Life" (John 6:48).

Bread as gift has always been popular. After Abram successfully beat off some evil neighboring kings and rescued Lot, King Melchizedek broke out bread and wine for thanks (Gen. 14:18). Jesse sent a donkey-load of bread with his son David to Saul, along with the boy's harp to play Psalm 23 to that bipolar king (1 Sam. 16:19). When King David fled to the wilderness to escape his evil son Absalom's conspiracy, Ziba, the steward of Mephibosheth came to him secretly with a string of donkeys loaded with two hundred loaves of bread (2 Sam. 16:1).

Our family, too, has given bread as gifts. A daughter reluctantly took a home-baked loaf of whole wheat and honey bread to her school teacher for a Christmas gift, instead of the customary cheap perfumes made for such occasions. Another daughter, as adult, and much addicted to her newly bought bread machine, gave us square loaves of pumpernickel, rye, and onion. As a professor of young off-beat poets, I've received my share of breads from male students, their self-made loaves as tough as their young bodies. One at first ate at it gratefully, full of honor; later set it aside, and by week's end abandoned it.

My wife's pioneer missionary mother in remote Tanzania in the 1930s baked bread in an earthen oven she formed by scooping out a bowl-shaped pit in the ground. Heating the indentation with charcoals, then, setting in the pan of bread dough, she'd cover it with hot coals on a lid, and guessed at her oven's temperature and time needed. She kept her family in bread; they rose up to bless her.

With so many bread stories in Mark—and more to come, real and symbolic, one should salute the Breads of the World. I pull down from our shelf of cookbooks a most unusual collection of recipes: *Extending the Table: A World Community Cookbook*, produced by the Mennonites of the world. Here, then, a short roll call of world breads:

Injera—Ethiopian flat bread: A two-foot circle of spongy crepe-like bread made from a three-day fermented batter.

Chipati—Indian flat bread: Of varying sizes and thicknesses in Asia and Africa, a useful scoop for curries.

Puris—Indian whole wheat bread puffs: Deep fat fried, they puff and rise to the top of the oil. A snack or with a sauce.

Khubiz Arabi—West Bank pita: A Middle East staple, its pocket stuffed with chopped vegies or pureed hummus.

Arepas con Queso—Colombian hominy cheese patties: Made from local maize, a common substitute for wheat breads.

Tortillas de Harina—Mexican flour tortillas: Made of wheat and corn flour, dry looking, but soft and pliable.

Bannock—native Canadian biscuit bread: Good stuff to pack for days of trapping, berry-picking, or rice-harvesting.

Diphaphat—Botswana stove-top muffins: Yeasty, tasty, round, heavier than an English muffin.

Paska—Ukrainian Easter bread: Mennonite immigrants to Canada from the Soviet Union brought this recipe; iced with vanilla-flavored minced egg yolk and cottage cheese.

Barm Brack—Irish Raisin bread: A hearty tea bread, delicious toasted.

Schwartzbrot—Austrian sourdough rye bread: Sour, thick, chewy, crusty.

Finally a dozen more common breads from which to draw life: hot-cross buns, sugarplum rings, baguettes, croissants, crepes, brioche, bagels, Danish, Italian, southern biscuits and corn pone, pumpkin-cranberry-pecan-banana breads—not to mention America's favorite lunch box bread, airy bleached white wheat squares for pale bologna sandwiches.

Just as Jesus said, "I am the bread of life," he could also have said, "I am the Bread of the World." To all bread-eaters of the world, he says: "Take of me, and eat."

Men Like Trees Walking
The Healing of a Blind
Man at Bethsaida

*At Bethsaida some people brought a blind man and begged Jesus to
touch him. He took the blind man outside the village. Jesus spit on the
blind man's eyes and put his hands on him. "Do you see anything?"
Jesus asked. "I see men like trees walking." Again Jesus put his hands
on the man's eyes. Then his eyes were opened. —Mark 8:22-26*

AGAIN, LIKE THE DEAF-MUTE AT TYRE, nothing is said about this
blind fellow's faith. Rather, it seems Jesus responded to the im-
portunities of the blind chap's friends. And again, like the deaf-
mute at Tyre, Jesus took his patient aside from the group for a
private consultation. Here Jesus "took the blind man by the hand
and led him outside the village."

Now about Jesus spitting on the poor bloke, we modern
readers are squeamish, even repulsed. Nor does it help much to
be told by eminent Middle East scholars that "the ancient world
had a curious belief in the healing power of spittle." Granted,
one does see a grandchild, sometimes even oneself as an adult,
pop a pinched finger into the mouth. The response is primitive,
intuitive, not something one learned from the American Medical Association's *New Family Medical Guide*. There I learn that
we humans have three pairs of salivary glands in our mouths:
under the tongue, on the floor of the mouth, above the jaws.

There, too, I read that "saliva functions as a lubricant and contains enzyme, a digestive aid, that breaks down starch." Who knows, some day a Nobel Prize for medical science might be awarded for a study showing the curative property of human spittle! And why not? I read in the November 1999 *Harpers Magazine* "Index" that the "percentage change since 1995 in the number of surgeons worldwide using maggots to cleanse wounds increased by 400!" Maggots, a medieval scalpel, now reintroduced into sterile and stainless steel surgery?

Outside of Jesus' use of spit I cannot find anywhere else in the Bible its positive use. But the use of spitting in one's face as a way of inflicting shame or showing contempt is recorded in Scripture, as a few examples will show:

When Miriam came out of the cloud "leprous like snow," her brother Moses implored God for her healing. The Lord's reply: "If her father had spit in her face, would she not have been in disgrace for seven days? Confine her outside the camp for seven days" (Num. 12:10-16). Moses gave this injunction for a man who didn't want to marry his brother's widow, to have children to her to carry on his dead brother's name: "Take off one of his sandals and spit in his face" (Deut. 25: 9).

In Isaiah's prophecy, the Suffering Servant submitted to abuse: "I offered my back to those who beat me; I did not hide my face from mocking and spitting" (50:6). This was then fulfilled in the gospeler's records: The irate Jews spat on Jesus at his trial before High Priest Caiaphas; the governor's soldiers spat on him at the crucifixion.

This short incident documents Mark's integrity as a carefully accurate reporter. Here is a gradual recovery of sight. At first try, with spittle and the laying on of hands, Jesus effects only a blurry vision. "I see men as trees, walking!" the blind man exclaimed (KJV). Had I had a holier mind I might stay it from thinking just now of the poor messenger who bears to Macbeth the news: "I looked toward Birnam, and anon, methought, the wood began to move. . . . Within this three mile may you see it coming: I say, a moving grove." Of course it is! Malcolm, son of slain King

Duncan, ordered his troops each to cut a bough. Hiding under these, they march on Macbeth at Dunsinane Castle.

"Once more Jesus put his hands on the man's eyes." Then they were opened and he saw everything clearly. I like to think the twelve witnessed this gradual recovery of sight. Jesus conducted on the man a kind of symbolic show-and-tell lesson. Later perhaps they were to understand it as symbolic of themselves, of their partial insight, their blurred understanding of just who was this radical Jesus they'd signed up with. After his resurrection, their eyes of faith were opened fully.

Coming to a more mature faith is not without pain. I remember Lionel who turned out fine features in my journalism class. In individual conferences over his papers, he treated me to a semester of stories about his coming to faith: a rebel son of a southern Presbyterian preacher, a prodigal on high school Friday night binge-drinking, a mocker of his dad's faith, a bright young man drifting between dumb jobs. Then came a summer when for a lark he went to a Jesus' People rally, and, in the parlance of the charismatics twenty years later, was "slain in the spirit." How well he wrote; bright, he became fluent in Spanish with mere college classes, without the aid of a crosscultural experience in Spain or south of the border.

The next semester I did not see him for months, until one day he strolled in carrying a spirit as slumped as his shoulders. "The light is going out," he said. "How do I get it back?" The easiest thing for me to have done? Give him what I call the old evangelical lie: "Jesus is fun!" Instead, I welcomed him to that battle of faith reserved for maturing Christians. Told him about the old saint who consoled C. S. Lewis with this hard saying: "As the Christian life proceeds, answered prayers tend to be rarer." But that is what faith is all about. The Voice, silent, clears our spiritual vision to have faith in God, not in our answered prayers granting spiritual hoopla!

Whose Christ? Peter's Confession of Christ

Jesus and his disciples went to the villages around Caesarea Philippi. On the way Jesus asked them, "Who do people say I am?" They replied, "Some say John the Baptist; other, Elijah." "But what about you," Jesus asked. "Who do you say I am?" Peter answered, "You are the Christ."
—Mark 8:27-30

IN THIS GENTILE SETTING NORTH OF GALILEE, among monuments to Roman imperialists who thought themselves gods, among the caves of old Greek pagan pantheists, away from the heartland of Jewish orthodoxy, away from the crowds who want a Jewish political king, Peter confesses Jesus as the Christ, the Messiah, the Anointed One. To confess this in such a context is at once fresh, reckless, and sobering. Peter's acclamation is qualified in Matthew's gospel by having Jesus declare that "this was not revealed to you by man, but by my Father in heaven." Here at the middle of Mark's gospel stands this great confession: "Thou art the Christ."

But who is Christ? What does it mean to have the Christ among us? That Peter himself did not understand the full character of this Christ or the full nature of this Christ's mission is evident by the next episode: He takes Jesus aside and rebukes him for predicting his death. Not only then but these two thousand years later the question falls across our studies when we say, "Thou, Jesus, art the Christ" but need also to ask, "Yes, but whose Christ?"

I read in John Howard Yoder's *The Politics of Jesus* many words about a Jesus as a social critic and an agitator, a drop-out from the social climb, a spokesman of a counterculture; about an argument which makes the radical Jesus and his teachings a relevant and normative model for contemporary Christian social ethics; about a leader who calls into being a new community made up by voluntary commitment, a visible sociopolitical, economic restructuring of human relationships; and much, much more that I embrace. Also I embrace those places, even while discussing ethics, especially a radical pacifism, where the author tips his pen to Jesus the Christ. "There is no difference between the Jesus of *Historie* and the Christ of *Geschicte*, or the Christ as God and Jesus as man."

Then I read John Dominic Crossan's *Jesus: A Revolutionary Biography*, the popular adaptation of his *The Historical Jesus: The Life of a Mediterranean Jewish Peasant*—a book meant for a lay dabbler in the readings of his faith. I am, after all, hardly a fellow member of the Westar Institute's Jesus Seminar of Duquesne or DePaul or whatever. Much appeals, much offends. I understand the limited scope of the book: not an apology for nor a negation of the Christian faith, but "an impartial account of the historical Jesus as distinct from the confessional Christ."

Stimulating stuff here for the mind in a daylight reading, but not much consolation for the heart when one lies awake in the dark night. Jesus gets dissected on three vectors of intellectual inquiry: crosscultural anthropology, Greco-Roman and Jewish history; literary and textual criticism. So we have Jesus, an illiterate peasant acquainted with an oral culture. A Jesus whose divine origins are "just as fictional or mythological as those of Octavius." A Jesus whose teachings show the coloring of the Greek philosophy known as Cynicism—involving not to doubt everything, as today, but a disciplined indifference to one's everyday culture values. "The historical Jesus was a peasant Jewish Cynic."

I also read in Friedrich Nietzsche's *Beyond Good and Evil.* I relish his attacks on the pious or merely churchy German middle-class Protestants of his nineteenth century; his reading of the French Revolution as "gruesome superfluous farce" contemplated "from a distance" by "enthusiastic spectators from all over Europe." But I am chilled when he dismisses "the faith demanded by original Christianity" (by Christ) as something close to the faith of Pascal, which resembles in a gruesome manner "a continual suicide of reason." Arguing that from the very start Christ demanded sacrifice, enslavement, and self-mutilation. Using sharp-witted phrases: "religious neurosis," "penitential spasm," "masked epilepsy," to talk about faith in Christ. I turn away, intellectually piqued but without an ethic, without a modicum of modesty about the possibility of transcendence. All is abrogation.

I turn to worship the Christ cloaked in the divine Godhead. I turn to the seventeenth century metaphysical poet John Donne's "Good Friday, 1613, Riding Westward." To a preacher-poet who acknowledges his fight against his intellectual skill at fashioning metaphorical apologies, until broken he can address:

> O Saviour, as thou hang'st upon the tree;
> O think mee worth thine anger, punish mee,
> Restore thine Image, so much, by thy grace,
> That thou may'st know mee, and I'll turne my face.

I turn to the closing chorus of Handel's *Messiah.* If I can no longer sing tenor, still I soar, my heart swelling with praise: "Worthy is the Lamb that was slain, and hath redeemed us to God by His blood, to receive power, and riches, and wisdom, and strength, and honor, and glory, and blessing." Turn, too, to Lloyd-Webber's "Requiem"—moved to tears by the boy singing "Pie Jesus"—merciful Jesus, and the Agnus Dei. "Jesus Christ, have mercy upon me, a sinner."

Humbly with my congregation on a Sunday morning I sing: "Christ, we do all adore Thee." In the evening, alone, I say to him, "Thou, Jesus, thou art the Christ."

Must, Twice
Jesus Predicts His Death

Jesus began to teach that the Son of man must suffer and be rejected
and be killed, and that he will rise again. But Peter rebuked him. Jesus
said, "You don't have in mind the things of God. If anyone follows me,
he must deny himself and take up his cross. . . . What can a man give
in exchange for his soul?" —Mark 8:31-37

BRIEFLY, IN PASSING, WE NOTE THE MATTER of titles. Peter had just
acclaimed Jesus the Messiah, the Christ. Here, immediately
after, Jesus refers to himself as "The Son of man." More than
modesty is present in Jesus' preference. Would it not be insuffer-
able arrogance for one—even the Son of God—to announce his
Messiahship? And unwise, in these confused, politically volatile
days? Let others discover that he is indeed the Christ; let them
through faith earn the right to make that pronouncement—even
if in secret, as Jesus commanded.

Mark records Jesus using *must* three times in this passage:
twice about himself—"The Son of man *must* suffer, he *must* be
killed;" and once about his disciple—"He *must* deny himself."
Some translations use "let," and "should" instead of "must." I
prefer the harshness of must, the obligatory imperative tone suggested by its connotation. How appropriate to diction and tone
is the choice of one word over another, that sweaty province of a
poet worth reading.

Which reminds me of the word *promises* in the closing stanza
of Frost's "Stopping by Woods on a Snow Evening." "The woods
are lovely, dark and deep, / But I have *promises* to keep. . . ." How
different would be not only the tone but also the meaning had
Frost written "business agreements," or "work," or "money matters to attend to." The cluster of pleasant, positive connotative
associations with the word *promises* would be negated by other
words so nearly synonymous.

Bonhoeffer in *The Cost of Discipleship* notes the significance
of Jesus' use of both "suffering" and "rejection": "There is a dis-
tinction here between suffering and rejection. Had Jesus only
suffered, he might still have been applauded as the Messiah. All
the sympathy and admiration of the world might have been focused on his passion. But in the passion Jesus is a rejected Messiah. His rejection robs the passion of its halo of glory. It must be
a passion without honor" (95).

So the suffering for Christ, for the Christian, is not like that
of the university's soccer players. The thrust of leg, the pivot on
heel, the mid-air twist, the side leg-to-leg skip, the backward
canter on toes, the high jump with arched neck and snap of head,
the slam of body-to-body, spike-to-shin, the sweat, even the
tears—playing for themselves and for their parents and sweet-
hearts in the bleachers, and their growling coach prowling the
sidelines. All this suffering, believes Bonhoeffer, has "its own in-
trinsic value, dignity and honor."

The disciple too *must* "deny himself and take up his cross."
Again Bonhoeffer: "Jesus makes it clear beyond all doubt that
the 'must' of suffering applies to his disciples no less than to himself. The disciple is a disciple only in so far as he shares in his
Lord's suffering and rejection and crucifixion. The first Christ-
suffering which every one must experience is the call to abandon
the attachments of this world" (96). And later, his famous epigram: "When Christ calls a man, he bids him come and die."
How do I, and all Christians serious about following Christ, find
out what kind of cross is meant for me, has my name written on
it, reserved for me? Soon, sometimes very soon, one begins to

discover the shape and texture of that cross meant for him or her to carry.

My mind turns to the cross in art, architecture, iconography—and costume jewelry. Early the Christian church adopted the cross as a sacred symbol, an icon, that expression in art of an idea, a person, or an event. While the Roman and the Orthodox (Greek, Egyptian, Syrian, Russian, Coptic) first imprinted a dominant form, down through the centuries came hundreds of variations. Also, during the High Renaissance in Italy and the following Baroque period, the cross became the floor plan for church and cathedral, with its nave, narthex, apse, transept, and so forth—which one senses, whether standing in St. Peter's Basilica, Rome, or the Mexico City Cathedral. The cross, ornate with gold and silver, rises above the ciborium of the Mass; it rises in my simple Anabaptist church at Easter. Some sister weaves a wreath of naked rambling rose stalks with their blood-red thorns and places it with a scarf of purple and a pot of white lilies at the base of a plain wooden cross.

Two crosses hang in my home. One is Ethiopic, bought years ago on a visit to friends in Addis Abba, sighted in a gift shop after a tour of the Ethiopian Coptic Cathedral. We could afford no silver or intricately carved three-foot cross; ours of rusted metal might be made from a spring of a 1930s vintage Italian Fiat. The other cross is Celtic, basically a Latin cross with a thick ring about the intersection of the cross bar and the upright shaft, made of reconstituted reddish gravel-grit. This cross is a gift from a former student on a spiritual quest who spent a semester at the Iona community. That summer when Phil took youth on week-long climbs into the California High Sierras, I touched it daily with prayers for his safety.

Now about the crosses people wear. I see them nestled in a mat of cinnamon hair on the bronze chests of jocks and dangling from young women's ears as daintily curved and translucent as a chambered nautilus. Something has happened I do not care for: the instrument of shame and suffering is now a tasteful accessory.

Shut Up!
The Transfiguration

Jesus took Peter, James, and John up a high mountain. There he was transfigured, his clothes dazzling white. Elijah and Moses appeared and talked with Jesus. Peter said, "Let's put up three shelters." (Peter did not know what to say. . . .) A Voice said: "This is my Son, whom I love, Listen to him!" Then, suddenly, the disciples looking around, saw only Jesus. —Mark 9:2-13

I SHOULD BE WRITING ABOUT DAZZLING white clothes, "whiter than anyone in the world could bleach them." Or about a Voice declaring Sonship, or about that Son binding his disciples to secrecy. Or about a special favor for a special three. But I am distracted by the stuff in the parenthesis. ("Peter did not know what to say. . . .") I laugh at Mark's need to apologize for the big mouth among the twelve. If Peter didn't know what to say, why didn't he just keep his mouth shut?

We all know people like him, some are close friends, some sleep in our houses during family reunions. I would not want to go with Peter to a Bach Festival. In the middle of the tenor Evangelist's limpid solo in "St. Matthew Passion," Peter would turn to you and whisper how goose-bumpy that man's voice turns his flesh. He'd insist that you feel him; if you resisted, he'd force your hand to his bared goose-fleshed arm. You'd miss a heart-wrenchingly tender glissando in the tenor line, making note to never, never, never again sit with this bloke at Bach!

In the previous incident, Peter declared Jesus the Christ; Jesus declared that he must suffer and die; Peter rebuked Jesus; Jesus as good as said to Peter: "Shut up, Satan!" Now here was Peter again, frightened, nervous, his big mouth blathering away, embarrassing James and John, who thirty years later still felt the sting of Peter's gooseyness when they related the incident to reporter Mark.

And it wasn't to be the last time Peter's jawing away got him into trouble. When Jesus was captured and taken to the Sanhedrin for an illegal trial before the priests, a wench of the high priest pointed a finger at Peter and said, "This fellow's one of those guys with the Nazarene." But Peter could not keep silent. He had to curse and swear and deny. "I don't know this man!"

Yet surely he knew the wise, lovely poem, "A Time for Everything," by King Solomon (or whoever): "There is a time for everything, / a season for every activity. . . . a time to be silent." And the little prophet Habakkuk's injunction, "The Lord is in his holy temple; let all the earth keep silence."

We live in a noisy time—from industrial machinery and human mass media. I wonder if anything has changed human nature so much as the loss of silence taken for granted. Not Gutenburg's press, not Einstein's atoms, not Armstrong-Aldrin's moonwalk. The voice of the machine is heard in the land day and night. Also technology gives us the human voice talking to itself day and night, on a hundred twenty-four-hour radio and television stations.

Chatter is an affliction even among the religious. How many university chapels and public worship services have I endured where "sharing" was esteemed worthy of our time, beneficial to our keeping covenant with the Living God.

When I heard one last worship leader say we would have "general sharing" this morning, I entertained myself with the notion of seeing four-star General Sharing, all strut and swagger, riding crop striking his leather boots, approach the podium in my peace church. Why have we been made to believe that the private stirrings in the soul need to be shared? That those who share are more virtuous? As though they've added "sharing" as an eighth to the Seven Cardinal Virtues? I agree with Nouwen in *The Way of the Heart*. "Let us at least raise the question as to whether our lavish ways of sharing are not more compulsive than virtuous" (38).

The saint, the artist, the writer, the ordinary man such as I need the silence, accompanied with solitude, for discovery and for growth. Even well-meaning institutions like churches and schools can inadvertently destroy the sanctity and need for solitude and silence. C. S. Lewis, writing a half-century ago in his essay, "Lilies that Fester," notes this inclination. "The educational machine seizes [the pupil] very early and organizes his whole life, to the exclusion of all unsuperintended solitude or leisure. The hours of unsponsored, uninspected, perhaps even forbidden, reading, the ramblings, and the 'long, long thoughts' in which those of luckier generations first discovered literature and nature and themselves are a thing of the past. If a Traherne or Wordsworth were born today he would be 'cured' before he was twelve" ("World's Last Night," 42).

"Why didn't you speak up?" my wife sometimes says to me with exasperation, following a congregational meeting or a public forum. I repeat what she's heard for years: "If I hear someone else arguing my position, I let him or her say it. Especially if they're more articulate on their feet, hold greater title or wealth, and still have good teeth and a thick thatch of ungrey hair." Years ago, during the social spasm of "letting it all hang out" to have integrity, I decided: I do not have to say everything to be honest. I can be silent, indeed, often need to be. What I choose to say, must be the truth. Not even all my good friends buy into this notion. My silence leaves them guessing: is he wise? is he a fool?

I think Jesus would have agreed with old Dutch philosopher Spinoza: "The world would be happier if men had the same capacity to be silent as they have to speak." Hey, Peter, shut up! You ruin a holy moment with chatter.

Belief and Unbelief
The Healing of a Boy
with an Evil Spirit

A man in the crowd said, "My son is possessed by a spirit. I asked your disciples to drive out the spirit, but they couldn't." Jesus said, "Bring the boy to me." The father said, "If you can do anything, take pity on us." "'If I can'?" Jesus quoted the father. "Everything is possible for him who believes." Immediately the boy's father exclaimed, "I do believe; help me overcome my unbelief." When Jesus saw the crowd running to the scene, he rebuked the evil spirit. Privately the disciples asked why they failed. "This kind comes out only by prayer." —Mark 9:14-32

SO, MAYBE NONE—NOT EVEN THE TEACHER?—can stay on in the eternal dazzle of light and snow-capped peaks of Mt. Hermon, at 9,000 feet, or Mt. Kilimanjaro, at 19,000 feet. I've never been to Mt. Hermon. But once I stood with Maynard and Donald in the ice fields of Mt. Kilimanjaro's peak, after a three-day hike. Climbing the last steep 3,000 feet in volcanic scree, light-headed from lack of oxygen, nauseous, I dozed, awaiting the sun rise. The dawn pinked, we looked down on a rolling ocean of clouds. I was transfigured—with hunger for air and food.

I wish I could report seeing a few old prophets, if not the Lord himself wearing Shekinah glow. Instead, I signed a book, my name lined below some European royalty, Count Somebody (perhaps Count Mippipopolous, the corrupt Greek out of the young Hemingway's *The Sun Also Rises*.) Then we went down the mountain, entered the clouds, and it snowed there, a few miles south of the equator.

Is no one to remain sealed in eternal mystical union with Christ? What do we say of those Greek Orthodox fathers locked on a tiny island where no woman has ever set foot, where even the goats are not female, as a silly rumor runs in the indignant protestant community. Should the monks in the Monastery of St. Catherine (dating from 330 C.E.), sitting at 5000 feet at the base of Mt. Sinai, also come out, come down, learn that solitary is for retreat, but not for life? That solitary is joined to solidarity, aloneness must be made one, solid with the human community? Or is all this only my Anabaptist distrust of an ancient spirituality that predates my own radical reformation of a mere five centuries ago?

The routine demands of the day await the spiritually transfiguring experience. From the high mountain country, where, as in Hemingway's *Farewell to Arms*, "it was clear, cold and dry and the snow was dry and powdery and the peasants took off their hats and called you Lord," down to the muddy Venetian plains and the Caporetto retreat, where the Italians lost 300,000, where stupid Italian officers shot their own frightened troops in a futile effort to turn them back on their Austrian-German enemy. From the clear snowy rapture on Mt. Heron to the dusty market place and a demon-possessed boy. A mere boy!—still saved from the sin-soured soul of his father. Indeed, "Suffer the little ones to come—"

The parent-child-faith-disbelief axis of this story snags the heart of any father who has a son, any mother of a daughter. Epilepsy. Seizures. It tears at a parent to see a child suffer. The father was desperate. He'd just experienced the powerlessness of the disciples (not the last to get no healing in a religious community). No wonder the father's request carried the conditional "If you can." Jesus' echo of that phrase in the negative, "'If I can'?" seems harsh. Even the conditions for the son's health seem a cold challenge: "To him who believes, all things are possible. Your son's cure is connected with your ability to believe in me." Why place that burden on the father here? Elsewhere, Jesus healed people who expressed no faith.

This is not altogether a comforting word from the Lord—actually, a frightening, sobering word. My child's spiritual healing—his or her wholesome *shalom*—depends on me, the parent? This incident of a child cuts much closer than the healing of a friend; it's a matter of flesh and blood: father and son, faith and doubt. Yet "all things are possible," Jesus challenged. Act with a sense of the possible, the positive. Cast off doubts and a negative spirit.

Am I too often like the father who is like the twelve, "I/we do believe, help me/us over unbelief"? Am I also like the disciples? Men gifted by Jesus to perform miracles come up against a devil they can't budge; they are powerless to effect an immediate change. I do not mean to suggest I am a miracle worker. Only that often I have felt ineffectual, humbled. The British fiction student, the budding Creative writing poet who sought me outside the class or office, in the privacy of my home or over curry and rice at the Nepalese, confessed to the demon lovingly nurtured in their hearts. Sometimes I could do little more than confess my own sin of doubt. Once I said to a thirty-year-old man: "It doesn't get any easier with age; you may as well believe now." Ten years later I find myself thinking that, like the fumbling disciples at their attempted exorcism, how little I gave him.

But there is a truth to what Count Greffi (*Farewell to Arms*) says: "I had expected to become more devout as I grow older but somehow I haven't." It seems a rather desperate thing for a ninety-four-year-old fellow to ask of an ego-centered youth, "Pray for me." Yet for some, a truth. Believing does not get easier nor do we find ourselves more "devout" as we get older. Indeed I needed the prayers of my young students. The father's exclamation, "I do believe," is mine. The father's confession, "Help me overcome my doubts," is also mine.

WWJD
Who is the Greatest?
Little Children

*Jesus sat down, and taking a child in his arms, he said to the twelve,
"Whoever welcomes one of these little children in my name welcomes
me."... People were bringing little children to Jesus, but the disciples
rebuked them. Indignantly, Jesus said, "Let the little children come to
me, for the kingdom of God belongs to such."*
—Mark: 9:33-37, 42; 10:13-16

THOSE DAYS JESUS WAS UNDER A LOT of pressure, in the parlance of
the twenty-first century. Herod and High Priest were angry with
him. He'd set his face toward Jerusalem and dying. He'd instructed his disciples on serious matters about life in the new
kingdom. Yet he had time for children. Not just "quality time"—
that self-complimentary phrase with which two-income parents
grace the ten minutes they spend with their young ones between
dinner and bedtime—which in their hearts they know is too
often a self-serving lie.

Perhaps Jesus picked a precocious child like himself to set on
his lap. A child that "grew and became strong, and was filled with
wisdom, and the grace of God was upon him," as Matthew so
generously dotes on the boy Jesus (2:40). Perhaps he chose an
older boy, much like himself at twelve, hiding from his parents
for three days so he could sit among the scholars in the temple

court, asking questions, even offering wise insights beyond his years' experiences.

Perhaps Jesus risked taking on his lap that kind of a kid. But I think it unlikely. He wanted no distractions for his "show and tell" session. He chose a fat docile boy from a grandfather with a cane in his hand. It would be a scene out of Zechariah's vision. "Once again men and women of ripe old age will sit in the streets of Jerusalem, each with a cane in hand because of his age. The city streets will be filled with boys and girls playing there" (8:4, 5). He chose a gentle child like the boy Jesus the non-canonical tales relate: he modeled clay pigeons and breathed on them life, and they flew away. He was sweet to his sisters, did not pull on their braids, nor tickle them when they carried water pots. Chose a kid like the bland blond British children I saw at my Nairobi Swahili language school. They lay placid, smiling, their faces round and pink as good translucent porcelain.

I think it was Charles Sheldon with his *In His Steps* that first made popular the phrase: "What would Jesus do?" I remember the first young woman in British Fiction class wearing a WWJD throat choker. Day after day, until my curiosity got the better of my old-fashioned manners, and I asked about the initials. "Oh, this? WWJD? It stands for What Would Jesus Do?" She was pleased to give witness to her old professor, whose name she probably kept on a prayer list.

Reading this Mark passage again, I thought of WWJD and tried to imagine Jesus coping with some delightful, unsuppressible kids from the pages of my children's story books. What would Jesus do with Ralph, Imogene, Leroy, Claude, Ollie, and Gladys, those horrible Herdman kids of Barbara Robinson's "The Best Christmas Pageant Ever?" who were "absolutely the worst kids in the history of the world. They lied and stole and smoked cigars and talked dirty and hit little kids and cussed their teachers and took the name of the Lord in vain." And instead of bearing frankincense and myrrh to baby Jesus in a manger they toted up a ham, the welfare ham of the church's charitable works committee.

What would Jesus do with the turn-of-the-century, ten-year-old pixie, Virginia Carry Hudson in *O Ye Jigs & Juleps*? An Episcopal sprite who rounds up the neighborhood kids to play Baptist and supervises baptizing in Mrs. Williams' rain barrel; who yells "The Lord is in his Holy temple, keep silent and shut up"; who grabs poor baby Melvin by the back of his diaper to dip him three times for the Trinity into the rainwater barrel, whose safety pin breaks and he drops to the bottom of the barrel?

What would Jesus do with the kids from Harper Lee's *To Kill a Mockingbird* novel neighborhood? Motherless Jeremy Atticus Finch, his preschool reading sister, Scout, who shocks the family dinner decorum with a practice shot at swearing: "Pass the damn ham," and puny Dill, the seven-year-old next door summer neighbor kid—scaring themselves silly with stories about a haunted house?

What would Jesus do with our year-old toddler Maria whom Dr. Eshleman wanted on stage with my wife one night before 300 mothers to give an illustrated interview-lecture on coping with preschoolers? What would Jesus do with this child who had no devil to provoke but went wild before bright lights and would abide no doctor's lap or public soothing words but had to be rescued from a discombobulated speaker?

What would Jesus do with the children in Dylan Thomas' *A Child's Christmas in Wales*? Tough, bored, street-smart boys who roamed the village, writing in the snow "Mr. Daniel is a Spaniel," mailing snowballs through their neighbors' front-door letter slots, and swaggering with candy cigarettes.

What would Jesus do with a Huck Finn, Tom Sawyer, Pippy Longstocking, Romona Quimby; with third graders with head lice; with nice boys addicted to violent video games; with my two-year-old granddaughter Noa, a round, funny, sometimes stubborn kid who keeps all strangers at bay with shrieks?

To all of them I think Jesus would say, "Let them come." Even if later he'd have second thoughts about lifting just any child to his lap, even for a minute's sermon to his disciples!

A Cup of Water
Whoever Is Not Against
Us Is for Us

"Teacher," John said, "we saw a man driving out demons in your name. We told him to stop, since he wasn't one of us." Jesus said, "Don't stop him. No one who does a miracle in my name . . . is against us. . . . I tell you the truth, anyone who gives you a cup of water in my name because you belong to Christ will certainly not lose his reward."
—Mark 9:38-41

OF PARTICULAR INTEREST HERE IS JESUS' PHRASE, "a cup of water." His use of "cup" sets out a whole bevy of metaphorical mugs in Old and New Testament Scripture.

"My cup runneth over" (Ps. 23:5)—one's well-scrubbed daily mug of life is filled to overflowing with God's beneficence, God's grace and mercy (to use, for efficiency here, the abstract code language of faith!). The cup so runs over that we flow out as nourishment to others.

"I will lift up the cup of salvation and call upon the Lord," the poet-psalmist replies, answering his own query: "How can I repay the Lord for all his goodness to me?" (Ps. 116:13). Our golden chalice of worship, a drink offering, is raised before the Lord, drunk and poured out in blessing upon the earth.

Elsewhere the psalmist writes of the cup of bitterness: "fiery coals, burning sulfur, and a scorching wind, God will rain down on the wicked" (11:6)—a white-hot metal vessel of divine wrath, steaming, bubbling, to be poured "in that Day" on "the wicked who love violence."

"Cup of bitterness" reminds me just now of James Baldwin's short story "Sonny's Blues," which tells of two brothers, one a jazz pianist, the other a math teacher. The jazz brother is released from prison on a heroin charge. The teacher brother goes one night to a Village joint to hear his brother play. He has an epiphanic moment as he listens to his brother's music. "I understood, at last, that he could help us to be free if we would listen, that he would never be free until we did." He sends up to his brother on the stage a drink as a salute. Then, "just before they started playing again, he sipped from it and looked toward me, and nodded. Then he put it back on top of the piano. For me, then, as they began to play again, it glowed and shook above my brother's head like the very cup of trembling" (72). How right is that word *trembling* to end the story. Trembling—a word of ambiguity, for one trembles with suffering, with uncertainty, with hope.

Later, Jesus makes "the cup" a lasting spiritual significance. I do not know whether his metaphorical use is a metonymy or a synedoche—perhaps a bit of both? "This cup is the new covenant in my blood, which is poured out for you. . . . Drink this in remembrance of me" (Luke 22:20; 1 Cor. 11:25).

My interest is particularly pricked with Jesus' word *reward*. In summary, he declared this: The cupbearer of water to others will himself be refreshed. Anyone who blesses the followers of Jesus will himself get a blessing. This promise pleases me enormously! I think of a wife, the children, and those former students, who have borne to me refreshment and nurture, cold drinks from the sacred chalice of their own lives. Their words anointed my exhausted head, their deeds girded up the weary loins of my mind. While I could write of the hundreds of cups of cold water they gave me over the years, I must select only a few.

A watercolor by Michael. Five years older than the average university student, he had lived many lives between the two stints of college work. Since he had something to write about and was serious about writing it, I gave him particular attention. One day he brought to my home a winter scene he had painted. A filigree of bare black branches against heavy sack-like clouds, mauve and gray; a stone house, a stream purple with cold, a white snow fall, a silence, a Robert Frost poem of a painting. Michael had labeled it "Fragment of Soul II." He'd added an explanatory note: "Winter at Locust Ford Farm, Oley, Pennsylvania." And a further note saying that the watercolor was "not in payment or return for anything, and yet for everything."

An embrace and a kiss from the son. I'd read from my stories at a departmental dinner and reading. Later that night Lawrence dropped by the house. He told of one student saying how easy it must be for someone to write who has spent his whole life reading and writing and teaching writing and literature. He's wrong, of course, the son, a guitarist said. "Writing a story is like writing music. You spend hours to get a paragraph right, to get a set of chords the way one hears it in his head." It was a Joycean epiphanic moment. This young man is indeed my son. Composing on his guitar, he understands his father writing at a desk.

And Peter writing from Burundi: "The reason I want to pursue an academic career is not simply to get paid to read books and have summer to fish, all good reasons, but I wanted to be a professor, for other confused and scared kids—what you once were for me and some of my friends."

And more and more cups of water: a wife's steady hand when I thought I lay dying of a heart attack; congenial and supportive colleagues; the children's party thrown for me on retirement from the university classroom; the warm letters and visits from a dozen former students. May they all and those I have no space to name, all who once bore me a cup of celebration, receive a cup of refreshment in their day of need—if not from me, then from someone who knows them, who loves them.

Go to Hell
Causing to Sin

If your hand . . . if your foot . . . if your eye causes you to sin. . . cut it off. Better to enter the kingdom of God with one than to have two and be thrown into hell, where the worm does not die and the fire is not quenched. —Mark 9:42-50

ONE NEEDS TO DO A HARROWING OF the hell in the Old Testament and New to turn up the evolving idea of eternal damnation among those ancient Jewish writers, prophets and poets. As well as contemporary commentaries, geographies, and dictionaries. By "harrowing" I mean both its archaic and agricultural definitions: to torment and plunder; to cultivate soil with an instrument of spring teeth or disks; to wrest hell's roots from their historical place, and to refine hell's clods into a metaphorical or literal place.

Hell—a biblical translation of the Hebrew *Sheol* and the Greek *Hades*. An idea evolving from a shadowy abode of departed spirits to an elaborate cosmology of a place with unspeakable terror and pain, a den of hellish torture, a kind of flip canvas of Hieronymus Bosch's "Garden of Earthly Delights."

Gehenna—a New Testament Greek name for the Valley of the Son of Hinnom, a steep scarp of rock southwest of Jerusalem. A place of horrendous evil in the name of God-worship.

It started during the golden era of King Solomon. "On a hill east of Jerusalem, he built a high place for Chemosh, the detestable god of Moab, and for Molech the detestable god of the Ammonites. He did the same for all his foreign wives, who burned incense and offered sacrifices to their gods" (1 Kings 11:7).

Later came Ahaz King of Judah. "He made cast idols for worshiping the Baals. He burned sacrifices in the Valley of Ben Hinnom and sacrificed his sons in the fire." (2 Chron. 28:3). He is followed a few years later by King Manesseh, who "sacrificed his sons in the fire in the Valley of Ben Hinnom, practiced sorcery, divination and witchcraft, and consulted mediums and spiritists" (33:6). But good King Josiah, in renewing the Covenant with the Lord, "desecrated Topheth, which was in the Valley of Ben Hinnom, so no one could use it to sacrifice his son or daughter in the fire to Molech" (2 Kings 23:10).

Jeremiah swore this prophecy against Hinnom, declaring a word from the Lord: "People will no longer call it the Valley of Ben Hinnom, but the Valley of Slaughter, for they will bury the dead there until there is no more room. Then the carcasses of this people will become food for the birds of the air and the beasts of the earth" (7:31). A place where "worms will not die, nor fires be quenched." Thus Valley of Hinnom supplied the imagery for a later Gehenna—the Hebrew hell.

Hell suffers at the hands of theologians, medieval and contemporary. One can take any number of readings about hell in the New Testament. Here are four to choose from: (1) the eternal abode of physical and psychological suffering for evil people; (2) a description of the eventual annihilation of the unrepentant wicked; (3) a holding pen in the hereafter for the unsaved whose suffering on separation from God purifies their souls and fits them for eternal bliss; (4) living is hell and at last, by the irresistible power of divine love and grace, all are fortunately saved.

Few passages in fiction match the preacher's sermon on "death, judgment and hell" in Joyce's *A Portrait of the Artist as a Young Man.* The school boys in a weekend spiritual retreat are treated to soul-chilling, concrete descriptions of the eternal damnation which awaits "my dear little brothers in Christ" if they persist in their sins. Aside from the masturbators, the only other sinner is Stephen Daedalus, who "will not serve home, fatherland or church."

"Hell is a strait and dark and fowlsmelling prison, an abode of demons and lost souls, filled with fire and smoke," the preacher begins in his first of three days of cold deliberations. "The fire of hell has this property that it preserves that which it burns and though it rages with incredible intensity it rages forever. Just as every sense is afflicted with a fitting torment so is every spiritual faculty; the fancy with horrible images, the sensitive faculty with alternate longing and rage, the mind and understanding with an interior darkness more terrible even than the exterior darkness which reigns in that dreadful prison" (119).

Today, the fearful edge of such language is blunted by the artificial stimulants of horror movies (which I do not attend—and I have yet to read a Stephen King novel) and TV talk shows hosting suburban witches sans conic hat and broomstick. For many, hell is a shopping mall at Christmas. Just yesterday my barber (I still cannot think of them as they prefer: hairdresser—which seems like a person attending a Thomas Jefferson powdered wig instead of my thinning brush!) said: "I'm dead sick of Christmas by December 3. Still out at the mall by then I think, Hell, isn't Christmas over yet!"

With the approach of the third millennium, in November 1999, *Newsweek* did its obligatory duty to write how the apocalyptic terror of end times shaped the world as it approached the year 2000. But we Americans seemed more afraid of our planes falling out of the skies at midnight year 2000 than we were of falling into hell. Only three percent plan on going to hell versus 68 percent to heaven. I suppose the other 19 percent believe in painless annihilation—or will still be out shopping in America's malls this Halloween for Christmas gifts.

On Becoming One Flesh
Avoiding Divorce

Some Pharisees tested Jesus by asking, "Is it lawful for a man to divorce his wife?" Jesus answered, "Moses wrote you a certificate of divorce because of your hard hearts. But God planned for one man and one woman to become one flesh. . . . What God has joined, let man not separate." Later, alone with him, the disciples queried further. Jesus said, "Any one who divorces his spouse and marries another commits adultery."—Mark 10: 1-12

I'VE HAD THE HONOR—AND ITS SUBSEQUENT burden—of being asked to speak at several weddings: of my three children, a nephew, a handful of former students. One soon runs out of fresh things to say about such an old institution, finds oneself tempted to cannibalize old texts, restate the obvious, even slip into the sentimental. I have found, too, that I have less practice, therefore less skill, at writing for the ear rather than for the eye. I learned to assume that while the mini-sermon is addressed to the bride and groom, neither is paying much attention. Her mind's on the obligatory satin and roses of a middle-class three-acre spread of gowns and tuxes. His mind is on that night's nuptial bed. So I wrote for the ear and saw that they got a copy of my meditation. Third day of honeymoon and bored, they could read it, hear "it again for the first time," to borrow a jangle from a seductive ad to come home to Corn Flakes.

Because of all that, I worked hard at writing a good epithalamion. Part of the pain for an honor well-done is to sit through dozens of wedding sermons and try not to remember how much better I did it. Fighting that pride of "mine was better," then giving up and just letting the conceit of inordinate self-esteem roll over me. Enjoy what it cost the old man of the bride for this spread, I would remind myself; wonder if the reception will be more than cashews and mints; make notes for another smart wedding sermon; confess these insipid sins.

To Will and Serita I said, "In rather breathless astonishment at his discovery of love, poet-preacher John Donne in *The Good Morrow* wonders what he and his wife did in their earlier lives. The sheer delight in each other's love makes, as the poet says, 'one little room.' Between them the lovers make, inhabit, and 'possess one world.' They are self-contained. The relationship is pure, simple, unencumbered. Two people looking at each other, talking and listening to each other, loving each other. Later, children will be clamoring outside the closed bedroom door. One loves them, too. Later, there will be parents dying in the next room. And one loves them, too. But for now, for this moment in the bridal chamber, this new good morrow to awakening souls, the making of the one little room is all that matters."

To Katrina and Mike I said, "Love and life and faith are like the fellow in the Lord's parable: he finds a treasure, then he buys the field. Love and marriage, like life and work and faith, are at once a blend of serendipity and deliberation, a blend of the gift to make valuable discoveries not even sought for, and the skill to weigh carefully before making a far-reaching decision. Going about your days' work, like the man plowing with oxen in the field who turns up a pouch of old Imperial Roman coins, you discover what is of value in life for a vocation. Then, like the man in the parable, comes planning, calculating, saving, denying, to lay hold on what came to you in a moment's illumination. Just now, it's buying the field in which you discover the treasure."

To Tim and Christine I said, "You'll remember that Dostoyevsky's *The Brothers Karamazov*—that 900-page novel of nineteenth century Russia—tells the story of three brothers. Alexei, the youngest, a spiritual boy with a tender conscience, is studying at the local monastery when the saintly elder dies. Alexei vows to keep the night vigil as a monk reads the account of a wedding at Cana. But he dozes off and dreams that he's a guest at the wedding. Even though lulling asleep, Alexei hears in the words of this gospel story his commission: 'Do it. . . !' Do what? 'Give happiness to some poor people, people so poor they haven't even enough wine for a wedding.' Alexei then recalls his last conversation with the dead elder: go out into the world, bless your life, make others bless their own lives. As it was with the bride and groom at Cana so here today: the love they bear for each other helps them grow in love for the troubled world, outside their marriage, outside the monastery."

To Julie and Roy Dale I said, "The stream of your pleasant lives now pitches you on to new shores. Here you'll taste a new temptation, to accord yourself the privileges of North American capitalistic affluence, long sanctioned as your rightful Protestant heritage. In the end, what will all your life's energies have been worth expending? That which your good families and friends value: health, peace and justice, hard work, honesty, compassion, loyalty, kinship, books, music, gardens, a dry basement, silence, and above all, the life of Christ lived in community. And also good sex. I quote C. S. Lewis: about the time we think we're spiritual beings, there's the sudden sexual twitch that reminds us we're also physical beings. 'We are composite creatures, akin on one side to the angels, and on the other, to tomcats.' It's a bad thing not to be able to take such a joke. Worse, of such a pious spirit not to take a divine joke."

If marriages are still made in heaven, it still takes earthly flesh to keep them.

....

All About Bucks:
The Rich Young Man

A young man fell on his knees before Jesus. "What must I do to inherit eternal life?. . . I've kept all the commandments since a boy." Jesus looked at him and loved him. "Go sell everything you have and give to the poor." The young man went away sad, because he had great wealth. Jesus said, "How hard it is for the rich to enter the kingdom of God!" The disciples, amazed, asked,"Who can be saved?" Jesus said, "All things are possible with God." —Mark 10:17-31

WARNING! THE STYLE TODAY IS ELLIPTICAL; the tone, eclectic; the structure, juxtapostional; the mind subliminal, a stream of consciousness—as I think about money, wealth, money, a wealthy but sad young man, money, investments, money, tithes and gifts, money, and more.

So Bill Gates set up a one-billion dollar fund for the university training of African-Americans. So what does he do with the other nineteen billion?

On the eve of retirement I met with my financial adviser, and he talked about "my estate"—as though I have several farms among the hinter piedmont of Rockingham County. I grinned, enjoying the joke, expecting on his second use of "your estate" to see him throw himself back in his padded leather chair, roll out a belly laugh, and slap his thigh. On his desk lay the pitiful pile of monies garnered from a life's work of teaching in a church-related university, after a six-year stint of overseas voluntary mission service. When he did not laugh, I sobered over the charts and life-expectancy figures and was tempted to teach for another decade.

"Command those who are rich in this present world not to be arrogant nor to put their hope in wealth. . . . Command them to do good, to be rich in good deeds, and to be generous and willing to share" (1 Tim. 6:17-19).

Among Old Testament Jews, conventional wisdom held that wealth was proof of excellence of character and favor of God. If a family was rich, the neighbors as well as the priests believed their wealth to be a mark of divine approval.

An Associated Press story dated Charlottesville reports that the University of Virginia, one of my alma maters (how many academic mothers does one need in life!) gives a special review to undergraduate applicants with wealthy parents who may give money to the school. "Considering the families' ability to financially help the university seems to me to be a most legitimate admissions consideration," said the rector of the university's governing board.

Aristotle, the Greek philosopher—not the Greek shipping magnate—defines money as "All those things of which the value is measured by coinage."

A single, wealthy Christian woman across town eats alone at her $8,000 solid mahogany table; extended, it seats ten, more people than she has friends.

"When you have eaten and are satisfied be careful that you do not forget the Lord your God. Otherwise, when you build fine houses and settle down, and your silver and gold increase, and all you have is multiplied, then your heart will become proud and you will forget the Lord" (Deut. 8:11-14).

The Presbyterian pastor of John D. Rockefeller urged him to give away more and more of his wealth. Not privy to the pastoral call, I presume it had something to do with the welfare of Mr. Rockefeller's never-dying soul. But I always wondered, Did the good man of the cloth ever query just how ethically his parishioner gained such stupendous wealth?

"People who want to get rich fall into temptation and a trap, for the love of money is the root of all evil. Some people, eager for money, have wandered from the faith and pierced themselves with many griefs" (1 Tim. 6:9-10).

Some of my Anabaptist brothers fly to Las Vegas for a weekend of gambling. They give their winnings to the church or their favorite charity. Having never accompanied them, I do not know what they do when they lose. Perhaps they blame the devil, a charming bloke who hangs conveniently around the tables.

An Associated Press story datelined Washington says that "one quarter of Americans believe their best chance to build wealth for retirement is by playing the lottery, not by patiently saving and investing. Asked how much $25 invested weekly for 40 years at a 7 percent annual yield would amount to—fewer than a third guessed over $150,000. The correct answer is $286,640."

"The Lord made Job prosperous again, blessing the latter part of his life more than the first. Fourteen thousand sheep, six thousand camels, a thousand yoke of oxen, a thousand donkeys, and seven sons, three daughters" (Job 42:10-15). Additionally, "nowhere in all the land were there found women as beautiful as Job's daughters. He granted them an inheritance along with their brothers."

My closest brush with instant wealth came in 1959. The owners of a supermarket my father managed gave him a $1,000 Christmas bonus. Father gave it to me, a poor recent-grad teaching as a volunteer in Somalia. Recently, I asked an economics professor at my university what that thousand is worth in today's money. Mumbling over his inexact science he came up with $10,000.

I think of St. Francis of Assisi and Dr. Albert Schweitzer—each walking away from careers which would lead to the comforts of wealth.

The Bible offers no simple answer to wealth or poverty. So neither voluntary poverty nor enormous wealth are accurate indicators of spirituality?

Astonishment and Fear
Jesus Again Predicts
His Death

*They were going up to Jerusalem, Jesus leading the way, the disciples
astonished, while those who followed behind were afraid. He took the
twelve aside and told them: "The Son of man will be betrayed to the
chief priests. They'll condemn him to death and hand him over to the
Gentiles. They will flog him and kill him. Three days later he will
rise." —Mark 10:32-34*

TWICE BEFORE (8:31 AND 9:31) JESUS told his disciples what was to
happen to him in Jerusalem. Here, this third time, he detailed
the horror of indignity and brutality. Even with graphic description, his twelve still didn't understand, as we read in the next
episode. I am like them: astonished. Why must his politics ne-
cessitate his death? Even two thousand years of writing on the
meaning of Jesus' death does not fully quiet the mind's curiosity:
What if Jesus had not been crucified?

Are the gospel of St. Paul and the teaching of Hebrews on
"the sacrifice of Jesus once for all" mere theological spinnings to
explain the historical miscarriage of justice? Is the old Hebrew
cosmology of a Jehovah whose pure wrath necessitates placation
solely by blood sacrifice—from lamb to Jesus-Lamb of God—
the only way to back read the evolution of Jesus' life? Yet a liberal
theology which reads the Jesus story cut off from a St. Paul theol-

ogy leaves a gutless Christ. One thinks of Swineburn and his
"Thou has conquered, O pale Galilean; the world has grown
gray from thy breath."

In addition to an astonishment similar to the disciples, I
nurse another aspect of surprise. Is the cross of Christ just an inward experience of the self , as sometimes in Billy Graham re-
vivals? The existential subjective brokenness, renunciation of
ego of a Dietrich Bonhoeffer? But the cross just might be that of
John Howard Yoder, as argued in his *The Politics of Jesus*: "It was
not an inexplicable or chance event, which happened to strike
him, like illness or accident. To accept the cross as his destiny, to
move toward it and even to provoke it, when he could well have
done otherwise, was Jesus' constantly reiterated free choice. . . .
The cross of Calvary . . . was the political, legally to be expected
result of a moral clash with the powers ruling his society" (132).

Setting all that aside, my eye catches the interesting detail of
how this group walked to Jerusalem—a walk of eight to ten days?
"Jesus was leading the way," then his astonished disciples, then
the frightened ones followed after. My video shoot places Jesus
way out ahead of the group, often walking alone. Yes, he had ses-
sions of instruction along the way, but more often he walked
alone. His attempts at telling them what they're going to experience in Jerusalem had met with disbelief and rebuke. Better then
just to walk alone with one's lonely thoughts.

Lines from a poem come to mind. Alan Seeger, one of several
World War I poets (Rupert Brooks, Wilfred Owen) wrote these
self-fulfilling prophetic words:

> I have a rendezvous with Death
> At some disputed barricade,
> When Spring comes back with rustling shade
> And apple blossoms fill the air—
> It may be he (Death) shall take my hand
> And lead me into his dark land. . . .

Jesus too had a rendezvous with death; his disputed barri-
cade was in the palatial courts of the High Priest and Pilate. His

Father too took him by the hand to a place the father himself could not go—death being outside of his own immortal nature.

If my astonishment places me with the twelve, my fear places me with "those others who followed afraid" at the rear of that group of pilgrims going up to Jerusalem. I fear I cannot sustain musings on every aspect of Jesus' Passion ahead to write worthy reflections. Six of the sixteen chapters—twenty-five episodes, more than a third of Mark's gospel—deal with Jesus' last week. Granted, there are lessons about taxes, marriages, apocalyptical signs, tenant farmers, and withered figs during this week—still, a dozen episodes center on Jesus' passion. So I find myself tagging at the end, fearful. Fearful that I have not the imagination to engender fitting musings; that I lack the sanctity of soul to breathe new life into these passages for my own edification; that my suffering is so slight that I can sound no full fathom of Christ's sense of abandonment by a Father; that my sorrow for my insipid sins which he bears to a cross is so callow as to be of greater offense than their first commission.

Yet, here the list of episodes stands waiting, for me, for any reader:

The Triumphal Entry
The Lord's Supper
Jesus Predicts Peter's Denial
Gethsemane
Jesus Arrested
Before the Sanhedrin
Peter Disowns Jesus
Jesus Before Pilate
The Soldiers Mock Jesus
The Crucifixion
The Death of Jesus
The Burial of Jesus

Wounded Servant
The Request of
James and John

*James and John came to Jesus. "Teacher, let one of us sit at your right
and the other at your left in your glory." Jesus said, "Can you drink my
cup, be baptized with my baptism?" They agreed they could. "You will
indeed drink my cup." The other ten were indignant. But Jesus said,
"Whoever wants to become great among you must be your servant. The
Son of man came to give his life as a ransom for many.
—Mark 10:35-45*

JAMES AND JOHN—LIKE PETER—missed the point of Jesus' teaching
about life in his commonwealth. They could not conceptualize
an upside-down kingdom. They knew their history: the golden
era of King Solomon; the courtly entourage of King David. They
lived under the strut and glitter of Herod's regal phalanxes. They
could image King Jesus' occupation of the High Priest's mansion
in Jerusalem, perhaps even the imperial Roman palace at
Tiberias. They were confidants of Jesus, hand-picked by him to
witness his transfiguration before Elijah and Moses, to be, if only
momentarily, recipients of that "eternal weight of glory."

So what they had experienced once so fleetingly—the sheen
of glory on a mountain—they wanted to enjoy forever. They
wanted to sit by their king "in his glory." They wanted to serve

their king in the coming new order, to be a knight at his round table, a minister in his cabinet.

So, what's so terrible about their request? The indignation of their ten colleagues suggests these men too had on their minds rank and position in the new order Jesus would establish. After all, they weren't slouching toward Jerusalem, but sweating it. "Surely some revelation is at hand. . . . Surely its hour had come round at last" (Yeats).

"Can you drink my cup?" Jesus pulls down for the Twins of Thunder a common metaphor, a common cup. From the temple choir music, Jesus' imagery lifts two Psalms: 23:5, "My cup runneth over," and 75:8, "In the hand of the Lord there is a cup." Such were songs these men must have heard sung often, songs which used "cup" as metaphor for the whole of life experience.

"Yes, you will drink it!" Jesus promised them. One's mind jumps to the sponge dipped into the cup of wine vinegar at the crucifixion. Perhaps Jesus was thinking of that place where, ironically, these twins might also be elevated, one on each side of their Teacher as they requested, but there in ignominy and ironically, too, a place of dark glory. Instead, the twins will have run away. Two robbers shared that honor.

"Can you share my baptism?" Jesus used another metaphor for the manner in which life sometimes weighs us down, not with glory nor the common trivia of living, but by hardship, hatred, loss of friendship, ennui, weltschmerz, depression, the death of a spouse, a dead-end career, a civil war. Baptized—drowned—in grief.

I think of two water-baptism examples from Virginia Woolf's *To the Lighthouse*. From her bedroom Mrs. Ramsay hears "the monotonous fall of the waves on the beach, which . . . (sometimes) had no kindly meaning, but . . . remorselessly beat the measure of life, made one think of destruction." And later, spinster artist Lily Briscoe, a guest in the Ramsey summer house, abandons herself to grief, shouts aloud for her dear dead friend, Mrs. Ramsay. In that abandonment, Lily thinks of herself as stepping "off her strip of board into the waters of annihilation."

"Can you drink my cup? Can you share my baptism?" are questions about bearing the Lord's cross. In his classic little 1960s book on missiology, *Yes to Mission*, Douglas Webster lists the ingredients basic to our Lord's cross. "We may discern four, all of which play a decisive part in the passion narrative: the government, the ecclesiastical hierarchy, the mob, and Judas Iscariot. The government gave its permission and endorsed a miscarriage of justice; the Jewish leaders plotting against Jesus finally got their way; the multitude, whipped up by professional agitators, shouted 'Crucify him'; and Judas . . . delivered Jesus into the hands of his enemies. So the cross of Jesus was made for him by the state, the church, the people, and a friend. These are still the powers which create innumerable crosses today for those engaged in mission" (106).

"You must be a servant." Without complaints, without being miffed by the master's orders, expectations and lack of thanks, without setting your own agenda, to borrow a contemporary image. A servant, faithful as the dog poignantly described by its prayer in Carmen Bernos de Gasztold's *Prayers from the Ark*. The dog imagines that only it and God "understands what faithfullness is." Pats, bones, even kicks do not matter. "I keep watch!" the dog reports and ends its prayer with a plaintive request: "Do not let me die / until, for them, / all danger is driven away."

I Want to See!
Blind Bartimaeus
Receives His Sight

*Jesus and his disciples, together with a large crowd, were leaving Jeri-
cho. A blind man, learning that Jesus was in the crowd, began shout-
ing, "Son of David, have mercy on me!" Jesus stopped and said, "Call
him." So they said to the blind man, "Cheer up! On your feet! Jesus is
calling you!" He ran to Jesus, who said, "What do you want me to do
for you?" The blind man said, "Rabbi, I want to see!" Jesus said, "Go,
your faith has healed you." Immediately Bartimaeus received his sight
and followed Jesus along the road. —Mark 10:46-52*

JERICHO: THE SETTING FOR THIS HEALING attracts one's attention:
layers of ancient civilizations lay beneath its foundation; centuries of history mark its significance; stone-walled wadis and
heat-impacted, below-sea-level temperatures shape its topo-
graphical geography.

Jericho: ten miles northwest of the Dead Sea; 825 feet below
sea level; a place of summer climate in winter; fifteen miles
southwest lies Jerusalem at 2,300 feet above sea level; so that in
those few miles the road drops 3,100 feet, twisting through
harsh mountain and ravine from Jerusalem to Jericho.

Jericho: the first city the Israelites have to demolish, newly
arrived in the Promised Land, in one of the oddest military
strategies ever employed. They blew ram horns, marched silently

around the city once each day for six days, seven times on the seventh day, then shouted, and the walls fell down. Two men grabbed Rahab the prostitute from the slaughter before they torched the whole city.

Thus, the Negro spiritual, "Joshua fit the battle of Jericho, Jericho, Jericho, and the walls come a tumblin' down." Long I thought the word "fit" meant that here was a battle which suited Joshua comfortably. Later I learned "fit" was the past tense for "fight" in colloquial English, particularly black slave. Still I rather liked the fit of my own misunderstanding.

Jericho: site for the passing of the mantle from Elijah to Elisha, where the new prophet performed one of his first miracles. With a bowl of salt he healed the brackish water of the town's well and thus inspired the first biblical record of a water softener.

Jericho: during Herodian times Romans built here their winter castles, the climate that far below sea level tropical. Excavations have uncovered mosaic floors, wine cellars, baths. More digs date flints, colored tile floors, pottery shards, and grain jars as far back as the ninth millennium B.C.E.

Jericho: here tubby tax collector Zacchaeus, "a wee, wee man climbed a sycamore tree for the passing Lord to see." Here, too, Jesus sets his short story, "The Good Samaritan." Since one dropped 3,100 feet in fifteen miles, little wonder he opens with "A man was going *down* from Jerusalem to Jericho."

Among the crowds gathering to go up to Jerusalem to keep the Passover celebrations was blind Bartimaeus, who wouldn't stop his bellowing to attract Jesus' attention. Having gotten it, he responded to his friend's call, "Cheer up! Jump up! Jesus is calling you!" His response was immediate—he ran to Jesus. His request was direct—"I want to see!"

Again, no catechistic examination. His persistence alone was an expression of faith sufficient. Jesus acknowledged that publicly with "Your faith has healed you." Here in ancient Jericho, Jesus did a fresh thing.

"I want to see!" That phrase bridged me into Thorton Wilder's "Our Town," possibly the best-loved play in modern

American drama, during my early years of teaching high school English. Poor Emily Webb, dead in her youth, longs to return to Grover's Corners, New Hampshire. "I want to see it all again!"

Granted her wish, she calls softly but urgently, "Oh, Mama, just look at me one minute as though you really saw me." Failing in that, Emily looks about the town at its routine living. "I didn't realize. So all that was going on and we never noticed." Implying blindness. "Do any human beings ever realize life while they live it?" To her query the Stage Manager replies, "No, maybe the saints and poets—they do some." To which Emily, exhausted, replies: "That's all human beings are! Just blind people!"

"I want to see!" The blind man's words have often been my prayer. Often, too, I've heard it said in private, in some fashion, by a dozen university students. Often it takes near-catastrophe for some to see.

Often I've turned them to Viktor Frankl's wisdom shaped by three years in Auschwitz, summed up in two paragraphs in *Man's Search for Meaning*, something I first read over thirty years ago. "I wish to stress that the true meaning of life is to be found in the world rather than within man or his own psyche. By the same token, the real aim of human existence cannot be found in what is called self-actualization. Human existence is essentially self-transcendence rather than self-actualization. Self-actualization is not a possible aim at all. . . . We discover meaning in life in three different ways: (1) by doing a deed; (2) by experiencing a value; and (3) by suffering." The second way of finding meaning in life is to experience work, nature, culture, love, faith. About suffering: one has the "freedom to choose one's attitude in a given set of circumstances" (157).

Blind Bartimaeus, eyes now opened, found meaning in following Jesus to Jerusalem. Together they would experience there a cataclysmic shift in human history.

A Borrowed Ass
The Triumphal Entry

As they approached Jerusalem, Jesus sent two disciples to find a colt. "If anyone asks you, tell him, 'The Lord needs it.'"... When they brought the colt to Jesus and threw their cloaks over it, he sat on it. Many people spread cloaks and branches on the road. They went ahead and shouted, "Blessed is he who comes in the name of the Lord!" Jesus entered Jerusalem and went to the temple. He looked around at everything, but since it was late, he went out to Bethany. —Mark 11:1-10

THROUGH TWO STONE-BUILT SUBURBS, Bethphage and Bethany, down through the Mount of Olives, Jesus arrived in Jerusalem. His first visit is recorded by Mark, but not his first. John has Jesus showing up regularly in Jerusalem for religious festivals. Once he cleansed the temple of livestock and money changers. Once he cured a thirty-eight-year cripple lying by a pool at Sheep Gate.

Nicodemus, that member of the Jewish ruling council who came to Jesus at night, surely was a resident of Jerusalem. Martha, Mary, and Lazarus, three of Jesus' intimate friends, lived in a Jerusalem suburb. And how often had Jesus climbed into the hillside of olive groves to weep? "O Jerusalem, Jerusalem, how often I have longed to gather you as a hen gathers her chicks under her wings."

Riding the young colt of a donkey in a procession strikes the Western mind as a rather silly mount. For a parade one wants a high handsome horse: a Tennessee Walker, an Arabian Thoroughbred, a Lipizzaner; or a great stout war horse: a Shire, a Belgian, a Percheron or a Clydesdale. Something like Napoleon Bonaparte's white horse. But much has been made about Jesus' choice. The horse was a warrior's symbol, such as the Roman mounts seen around town. The humble ass was respected for its nimble surefootedness on rocky Palestinian trails, for its steadfast endurance.

I saw my first donkeys in Somalia. The domesticated ones on the Mussolini Boulevards of Mogadishu held steady against the horns of irate Italian colonialists in their midget Fiats. These were indeed the proverbial beasts of burdens. One saw them in harness and shaft to a thousand carts loaded with timber, barrels of sweet water (the city had Indian Ocean salt water on tap!), and colossal mounds of bagged charcoal. From under mountains of harvested tall wild river grass, cut for city cows, only the donkey's lady-thin-ankles and a long sad face hung out.

Their wild ass cousin, with light residual stripes of an ancient evolution from the zebra, seen on Somalia's interior plains, brought to mind God's use of them to scorn Job. "Who let the wild ass go free? Who untied his ropes? I gave him the wasteland as his home, the salt flats as his habitat. He laughs at the commotion in the town; he does not hear a driver's shout!" (39:5-8).

What one rides or drives always makes a statement in our car-mad Western society. Many a young man's fear of lacking adequate sexual equipage is quieted with a fast sleek red sporty coupe. As it is for his heavily domesticated middle-aged bureaucrat father. Our vehicle declares "our relentless pursuit of perfection," "a synergistic relationship" between oneself, travel and the road; with the twenty-four-hour satellite Global Positioning System, one has a troubled fingertip if not God, a human voice, to offer guidance. If not a sleek sedan, then an SUV. My neighbor said, "You buy a car and drive it till it dies." A young man dating my daughter said, "Your dad will persist in driving that old car even if he can afford two new ones!"

So Jesus' choice of a mount was a deliberate, planned, use of a symbol. As was his whole triumphal entry into Jerusalem. He chose the day, the town filled with tens of thousands of people, many from the international jet-set. He chose his conveyance. He rode a colt common to the streets of the Old Towne, a colt prearranged with a friend to be used on the eve of the Passover, the pass-word-phrase agreed upon: "The Lord hath need of it." He waited to mount until the colt was cloaked, he waited until palm and olive branches strewed the street, he allowed himself to be paraded by a crowd rushing ahead and singing "Hosanna!" and "Blessed is he who comes in the name of the Lord," words from temple singers and prophets and old glory stories.

That Jesus staged his own entrance into Jerusalem troubles me not. His triumphal entry is great theater, great pageantry, great spectacle. My heart rejects John Dominic Crossan's dismissal of the event as "too much suspect for me to build on as a historical event. . . . I do not think that it ever actually happened, except as later symbolic retrojection."

Jesus did not swing the cheering crowds to storm the Roman garrison; he did not want another bloody Zealot revolt, another Bastille Day in Jerusalem. There he would have been a knight-errant-warrior-Messiah. Instead, he rode on to the temple. And the crowds knew to sing: "Rejoice greatly, O daughter of Zion: shout, O daughter of Jerusalem: behold, thy king cometh unto thee; he is just, and having salvation; lowly, and riding upon an ass, even upon a colt, the foal of an ass" (Zech. 9:9).

Entering the temple, Jesus looked about. Now in his Father's house, he must be about his Father's business. A strange silence fell over the courts that night. The crowds seemed suddenly to have dispersed. In the end, were only the twelve to witness the Lamb readying himself for the temple's altar? For a Roman cross?

A Slipped Fig Leaf
The Withered Fig Tree

The next day, leaving Bethany, Jesus was hungry. He saw a fig tree with nothing but leaves, because it was not the season for figs. "May no one ever eat fruit from you again." The next morning they saw the fig tree withered from the roots. Peter said to Jesus, "Rabbi, look! The fig tree you cursed has withered!" —Mark 11: 12-14; 20-26

THE PLAYFULNESS OF CHRIST'S SPIRIT is on me as I sit stewing on this fig of a story. But first I should attend to a few factual matters about figs, fig leaves, dressers of sycamore-figs and fig/fica, before not giving a fig.

In the higher elevations of Palestine grow two types of figs: the *Ficus carica* and the *Ficus sycomorus*. With this latter—the sycamore-fig—we associate Zacchaeus and Amos. Zacchaeus, wealthy, chief tax collector of Jericho, short-legged, had to climb a sycamore-fig to catch a glimpse of Jesus, so thick was the crowd enroute to Jerusalem for the Passover (Luke 19:4).

Meanwhile Amos, a minor prophet yet one with a major word from the Lord for Israel warned, "Your sons and daughters will fall by the sword; you yourself will die in a pagan country." For this he was scorned by the priest of Bethel, who told him to "go back to Judah and prophesy there."

Amos defended himself with a mixture of pride and humility: "I was neither a prophet nor a prophet's son, but a herdsman and a dresser of sycamore figs" (7:10-17). "Dressing" his sycamore figs, Amos made a small incision in the inch-long fruit a couple of days before harvesting them to speed their ripening. Either that or he may have discovered the benefits of pruning trees.

An aside: writing these musings on the Gospel of Mark, I feel the weight of the task: I am without formal credentials; I have no theological training; like Amos, have attended no school for prophets. Thus I should feel the discomfort of farmer Amos in "the king's sanctuary." I trained only to be a teacher of college English—literature and writing. Yet what I have written "seems good to me and the Spirit;" I feel exalted in the task but sometimes also feel at sea, though in the end I feel safe among us laypersons. I do not write for theologs; let them look elsewhere for their spiritual welfare, have they a soul. "But I was going to say," like Robert Frost in his *Birches,* "when Truth broke in with all her matter-of-factness about the ice-storm"—I was going to say something about Palestinian figs.

Native to the Mediterranean region, figs were eaten by humans before they could write about eating figs. People eat figs fresh, preserved, dried, pressed into cakes. A poultice of figs the Prophet Isaiah ordered applied to a boil saved King Hezekiah's life (2 Kings 20:7). The thirty-foot trees with their large leaves made copious shade, a place for rest from the searing sun, as attested to in Micah's vision: "In those days . . . nation will not take up sword against nation. They will beat their swords into plowshares. Every man will sit under his own fig tree" (4:2-4).

Old mother Eve quickly sewed up fig leaf aprons for Adam and herself when they became ashamed of their naked genitals after their fall from innocence (Gen. 3:7). And thus the first fig leaf brief was established, and would be revisited during later spasms of resurgent modesty.

John Ciardi declares in *A Browser's Dictionary: A Compendium of Curious Expressions and Intriguing Facts* that "whole generations of stonecutters were kept busy carving leaf addenda to the Greek and Roman genitals in the Vatican's enormous collection" of statuary. So the fig leaf, along with Constantine, was converted by Christianity, a bit of carved marble syncretism annealed to old pagan virulent exaltation of the flesh.

But Michelangelo's "David" of the Early Renaissance in Florence escaped fig-leafing. He—Mike, not Dave—touched that massive chunk of Carrara marble lying for fifty years behind the cathedral and released from stone an eighteen-foot nude David, sans fig-leaf. Its musculature—the body not the genitals, they are modest beside the massive right hand clutching a stone—is so lifelike it anticipates photographic realism. Granted, the genitalia unsheathed adds to the general pagan tone of Florence during that century, with a Florentine eye more to Athens than to Rome.

Not only from pagan Athenians, the Hebrews learned from the statuary of their pagan Syrian neighbors the vulgarity of a split hairy purple fig to signify a vagina, to make an obscene gesture by clenching the fist and thrusting the thumb between the first and second fingers. But for that, I "don't give a fig."

Nor for this gospel story about Jesus cursing a fig tree for being fruitless. The more so with Mark pointing out that "it was not the season for figs." This story lacks "the ring of truth," to borrow J. B. Phillips' phrase in reference to his translating of the New Testament. Nowhere did Jesus use his power for personal indulgence. Hungry after a forty-day fast, he would not command stones to become manna. Cornered by the enemy in Gethsemane, he did not turn flesh to stone to escape.

Nor do I give a fig for those commentaries which read the episode as "an enacted parable." A prophetic, symbolic, dramatic lesson for his disciples on the failure of contemporary Judaism to bear good fruit. Mark's excusing the tree for having no fruit ("it was not the season for figs") compounds the symbolic problems of the story; the Jewish nation, ancient and of Jesus time, should have borne all manner of fruits.

I think we should just admit that the old church fathers editing the sacred texts nodded off one muggy afternoon at their task. Or decided to risk this bit of noncanonical fiction to show the man side of the God-Man Jesus, to show that he could, when hungry, be as petulant as a Middle Ages monk without his daily mead.

. . . .

House of Prayer
Jesus Clears the Temple

Jesus entered the temple area and began driving out those buying and selling. He overturned the tables of the money changers and the benches of those selling doves, and wouldn't allow anyone to carry merchandise through the temple. "It is written: 'My house will be called a house of prayer for all nations,' but you have made it a den of robbers." The chief priests and the teachers of the law began looking for a way to kill him; they feared him because the crowd was amazed at his teaching. —Mark 11:15-19

> In Christ there is no East or West,
> in him no South or North,
> but one great fellowship of love
> throughout the whole wide earth.

I'VE BEEN PORING OVER CONJECTURAL floor plans of Herod's temple, the structure through which Jesus strolled. The temple precincts covered thirty acres on top of Mt. Zion. Four walls of 900-to 1,600-foot lengths enclosed the trapezoid space. One got inside these walls through an elaborate arrangement of arches, gates, passageways, which opened into porticoes, sheltered arcades, a rank of semi-circle steps for the choir, a guard house, galleries, and courts: for Gentiles, Women, Israelites (i.e. Men!), Priests. In the latter, their sacred furniture: the laver and the altar of burnt offering. Twelve more steps (one each for the tribes, one each for the disciples!) led to another porch, then the Holy Place displaying a massive candelabrum, the table of shewbread, the altar of incense. Then behind double curtains (veils which will be rent from top to bottom in another week) lay the dark and empty chamber called the Holy of Holies.

This temple, a place of worship, was unlike any Christian church—from your modest, suburban white-spired chapel to ornate St. Peter's Basilica itself—or a Jewish synagogue. Part of the temple worship was through animal sacrifice. So this messy and bloody work of slaughtering animals, burning parts in offerings, cooking and eating other parts had to be accommodated. Under the altar, a stone channel carried away blood and offal, and there were cisterns for water.

Tens of thousands of visitors went up for the high holy days. Not at all surprisingly, in the Court of the Gentiles, a kind of all-night convenience stop-and-shop sprang up to accommodate travelers who came too far to bring a home-raised lamb.

Further, at Passover, the annual temple tax had to be paid. Custom dictated that the Roman coins bearing the image of the detested Caesar-who-imagined-himself-a-god not be used. So Jews from Greece, Rome, Syria, Egypt, Phoenicia, Tyre needed coins that approximated the old Hebrew shekel. Perhaps the founding father of such a court imagined it a place of silence, for contemplation, to prepare the soul for a sacred encounter. Reading between the lines, one feels that by Jesus' time the atmosphere in this court was as secular, commercial, noisy with buying and selling, as any Arab or Egyptian outdoor market-place, as well as those of Africa in which I shopped for six years.

Just possibly there was nothing wrong with the buying, selling, money-changing in the outer courts, activities necessary for temple worship. But merchants and bankers couldn't stifle their instincts to turn a profit, even on holy days. Scholars tell us a pair of doves outside the temple precincts cost nine pence; inside the price doubled. Not unlike the price of a box of Jubies in a grocery and those in the movie salon. Turning a profit turned to exploitation to extortion.

Little wonder that Jesus threw a fit! It should have finally demonstrated to his disciples as well as the chief priests the point of his mission: his act of clearing the temple was a dramatically enacted parable about purging Israel of her sins; not to rid the country of Romans. He reminded his audience of their sins by citing texts from two of their prophets, Isaiah 56:7 and Jeremiah 7:11. "My house will be called a house of prayer for all nations, but you have made it a den of robbers."

I'm remembering the indignation of my seminary dean friend when his young son brought home from his public school a Gideon New Testament. An American flag was printed on the endsheet. The theologian, citing Jesus' words on cleansing the temple, tore out the page from the son's Bible. An act of righteous wrath against those who would make of God a civil religion. That the smoldering words of a Mt. Sinai God and the words of his lamb Jesus need endorsement by the red-white-and-blue flag of American businessmen! My memory tells me that he mailed the page with a note to the good Gideon fathers.

> Join hands, then people of the faith, whate'er your race may be,
> All children of the living God are surely kin to me.

"All nations, all people"—perhaps Jesus was also taking a cut at the walls that separated Gentiles and women from the Men's Court, nearest to the Holy of Holies! Perhaps, too, he was remembering the visions of those other prophets: "He was given authority, glory and sovereign power; all peoples, nations and men of every language worshiped him" (Dan. 7:12-14). Then Micah 4:1-3, "In the last days . . . the Lord's temple will be established . . . and peoples will stream to it. Many nations will say, 'Come, let us go up to the mountain of the Lord. He will teach us his way, so that we may walk in his paths.'"

> In Christ now meets both East and West,
> in him meet South and North,
> All Christly souls are one in him
> throughout the whole wide earth.
> —John Oxenham, 1908

Cheeky
The Authority of Jesus Questioned

While Jesus was walking in the temple courts, the chief priests, the lawyers and the elders asked him, "By what authority are you doing these things?" Jesus replied, "I'll ask you one question. Answer me, and I'll tell you my authority. John's baptism—was it from heaven or from men?" They discussed it among themselves then said, "We don't know." Jesus said, "Neither will I tell you by what authority I'm doing these things."—Mark 11:27-33

IT'S NOT SURPRISING, THIS QUERY FROM the chief priests, lawyers, and elders about the source of Jesus' authority. With a whip of cords, he had rather high-handedly purged the temple precincts of merchants, livestock, bankers, and foreign monies. But Jesus' response is surprising, a question which put the Pharisees on "the horns of a dilemma," a question which impaled them on both horns of a bull they'd rather not ride, a question whose either answer leads to defeat of an argument. Not unlike the query, "Have you stopped beating your wife yet?"

But it's the manner of Jesus' response, not his question, which delights us just now. Yes, you should turn the other cheek, as Jesus taught, but sometimes, as he shows us here, you just get cheeky and thumb your nose at the people in power.

The query about authority reminds me of Charles Baxter in the April 1999 *Harper's Magazine*. He tells of the intellectual, artistic, and athletic productions of the University of Michigan, Ann Arbor, of his colleagues who "rattle off facts and figures and concepts and patterns. The virtuosi of knowledge . . . their lives and their authority depend upon their ability to remember, and to remember their subjects in public. Having a private memory in a place like this might be pleasant, but it is certainly beside the point, at least professionally."

How true! How restful to enter retirement and lay aside the demand to flash one's professional authority in public. But having lost that, to know how little we in the West respect the wisdom accumulated by old people through experience and reflection. How little the Pharisees would respect the authority of Jesus borne of Sonship, rather than of a Jewish seminary. His answer seems cheeky. Occasionally we admire cheek in a person, particularly one bullied and despised by society.

Just such a cheeky person is Lucas Beauchamp in Faulkner's *Intruder in the Dust*. An old mulatto fixture in Yoknapatawpha County, he was bold with irreverence for the civil establishment: mayor, sheriff, lawyer, and the rigid white Southern mores. He was a descendant of Lucius Quintus Carothers McCaslin, an ancient white founder of a plantation, and McCaslin's black slave Eunice; on their half-caste daughter Tomasina, McCaslin fathers another child who is the mother of Lucas. Strong, haughty, dignified, old Beauchamp takes pride in his ancestry, black and white. This total acceptance of his black blood and white blood makes it impossible for the Southern townsfolk of the 1930s to pigeon-hole him. "Every white man in the county had been thinking about him [Lucas Beauchamp] for years: We got to make him be a nigger first. He's got to admit he's a nigger. Then maybe we will accept him as he seems to intend to be accepted."

So when a murder occurs, the townsfolk declare Lucas guilty. It will need to be a ritual lynching, each race "observing implicitly the rules." But Lucas did not shoot Nub Gowrie's son Vinson. Lucas actually knows who did. But he also knows that he, an arrogant old mulatto, hated by the town, cannot get any white male to believe his story. He calls and anoints sixteen-year-old Chick, a white boy, nephew of Lawyer Stevens, for that task. Lucas knows, as did old black Ephraim: "If you ever needs to get anything done outside the common run, dont waste yo time on the men-folks; get the womens and children to working at it. Young folks and women, they aint cluttered. They can listen. But a middle-year man, they aint got time, too busy with facts."

It will be Chick, his Negro boyhood companion Aleck Sander, and the near-eighty-year-old spinster Miss Eunice Habersham. They believe enough in Lucas Beauchamp's story to scorn white decorum, drive ten miles through the night in an ancient pickup, sneak into a rural graveyard, dig up the freshly buried coffin, and learn a truth the town doesn't want to hear. They not only have cheek, flaunted self-assurance, but true grit, and are just cheeky enough to guard Lucas from the gathering crowd of hill people who want to storm the jail and lynch him. Still wearing her hat and sitting in a rocking chair on the porch of the jail, Miss Habersham slips her darning egg into a sock and gazes into the yellow street-lamp night, her calmness the infuriating cheek of the righteous.

The outrageous cheek of an old mulatto, a youth, a black boy, and an old maid "brought into the light and glare of day something shocking and shameful out of the whole white foundation of the country which otherwise might have flared and blazed and then vanished back into its darkness or at least invisibility with the fading embers of Lucas' crucifixion."

It's high risk to be cheeky to authority, but sometimes it's the only moral authority left those who are weak. I feel moved to add another Beatitude: "Blessed are the dispossessed, for they can be empowered with cheek."

Sonship
The Parable of the Tenants

Jesus spoke to the Pharisees in this parable: "A man planted a vineyard. He walled it, dug a pit for the winepress, then rented it to some farmers. At harvest time he sent a servant to collect some fruit. They beat him and sent him away. Then another servant, and another, and another. The owner decided to send his son. 'They will respect my son.' But they killed him. What then will the owner do? Haven't you read the Scripture?" —Mark 12:1-12

NO LONGER JUST CHEEKY, BUT BOLD, Jesus told the Pharisees a story with a thinly veneered allegorical meaning. Now the Pharisees knew the Scriptures well, thus felt keenly the pinch of the allusion to them in Jesus' paraphrase of Isaiah's parable:

> My loved one had a vineyard on a fertile hillside.
> He dug it up and cleared it of stones and planted it with vines.
> He built a watchtower in it and cut out a winepress as well.
> Then he looked for a crop of good grapes,
> But it yielded only bad fruit.
> What more could have been done for my vineyard?
> Now I will tell you what I am going to do to my vineyard:
> I will take away its hedge, and it will be destroyed;
> I will break down its wall, and it will be trampled.

I will make it a wasteland, and briars and thorns will
   grow there.
I will command the clouds not to rain on it. (5:1-6)

But Jesus adds a line about the owner of the vineyard having a
much loved son. He decides to send him to the caretakers, because "They will respect my son."

And I thought of lines out of the second Psalm-poem, where
the speaker admonishes the rulers of the earth, "Kiss the Son, lest
the father be angry." If not here the kiss of affection, at least the
formal salute of obeisance to a sovereign. The kind of respect expected between ruler and subject, between land owner and the
renters. Respect me, respect my son; kiss me, kiss my son; love
me, love my dog.

Perhaps the vineyard owner thought of his son as "a chip off
the old block." Granted, the chip, whether off a block of wood or
a slab of stone, is in reality rather worthless. But we've used the
image for so long as to make it a rather sentimental idea of child
and father being of the same psychic stuff. About which John
Ciardi adds this rather sardonic observation: "I have known any
number of disastrous father-son teams to take great, mutual, stupid pleasure at being so likened."

I have a son and find this a fine thing. University students
who knew next to nothing about "my boy" nevertheless accord
him high respect solely because he is my son. Respect for the professor, respect for his children; love the old prof, like his kids—
well, at least without much thought, give them deference.

Once I opened a letter from an editor of a major Manhattan
publisher, expecting acceptance after six months of keeping me
in suspense with one-liner postcards of "almost, perhaps, any day
now." Only to find rejection. Without prompting, up surged
that line from Psalms 2: "Kiss the son, lest the father be angry
and destroy you." Ought not the modern New York pagan editor
give deference to the Lord's anointed writer? I wanted to ring
him up and cry, "Kiss the son, you heathen, lest Jehovah smite
you with dizziness!" (that last phrase from an Islamic curse I
learned in Somalia).

Why did the viticulturists imagine they could get away with killing the owner's son! Because, again, according to the poet-psalmist, "God was not in all [the evil men's] thoughts. They leave no place for God in all their schemes" (10:4).

Some days, God-haunted, God-hungry, I am envious—without fear, without guilt, without shame—of that person of which it is said, "God is not in all his thoughts." I think, What an absolute sense of peace such a wicked man, cleansed-of-God, has gained as he "crouches" in his "den," untroubled by any restraints. Why not relax? The Lord is "standing far off" (10:1). God is an absentee landlord; there is no need to kiss the son, out of affection or of respect. Like our modern secularists, the grape renters had learned how to live and die without a thought about God. So, shamelessly, they "killed the son and threw him out of his vineyard."

Ah, but that short, short story by Jesus, with its allusion to Isaiah's parable, made the Pharisees and company grind their teeth and look for a way to kill him. To be told, no matter how poetically, that they had made of Jesus the Stone of Rejection. Again they knew this allusion to the Psalter and the Prophet: "See, I lay a stone in Zion, a test stone, a precious cornerstone for a sure foundation; the one who trusts will never be dismayed" (Isa. 28:16). And, "The stone the builders rejected has become the capstone; the Lord has done this, and it is marvelous in our eyes" (Ps. 118:22).

The setting of stone for any old Anabaptists (if they know the sacred canon of their denominational history!) takes them to Mennonite founder Menno Simon's favorite verse, one with which he prefaced every pamphlet and sermon. "For no one can lay any foundation other than the one already laid, which is Jesus Christ" (1 Cor. 3:11).

Not that I am good or clever, but I thought of that verse when I stood before the gigantic cut stones in the southwest wall of old Jerusalem, stood among Hasidic Jews, praying at the wall, nodding in devotion, their ear curls bobbing. I did not kiss the Jewish wall, nor Catholic St. Peter's toe in the Vatican. Not squeamish, just that once I had kissed the real Son. Would these people, too, some day, "Kiss the Son"?

Now declare with the anonymous sixth century hymnist—

Christ is our cornerstone, on him alone we build.
With his true saints alone the courts of heav'n are filled.
On his great love
Our hopes we place of present grace and joys above.

As Sure as Death
Paying Taxes to Caesar

The Pharisees tried to catch Jesus in his words. "Teacher, we know you are a man of integrity. . . . Is it right to pay taxes to Caesar?" Jesus said, "Bring me a denarius and let me look at it." They brought the coin and he asked, "Whose portrait is this? Whose inscription?" They replied, "Caesar's." Then Jesus said to them, "Give to Caesar what is Caesar's and to God what is God's." —Mark 12:13-17

WITH THE UNCTUOUS FLATTERY AND false modesty of an arrogant Italian duke of the Renaissance negotiating a second marriage on the death of his duchess, the Pharisees and Herodians, strange theological bedfellows, set for Jesus a verbally baited trap. "Should we [Jews] pay taxes to Caesar?"

Were Jesus still in a cheeky mood, he might have rejoined, "Pax Romana doesn't come without a price. Pitch in; don't be a petulant puss!" After all, the Jews, too, experienced what all the Mediterranean lands, Asia Minor and the East enjoyed: tranquility and security for a length of time yet unknown. The provincial peoples of a dozen different lands found themselves free to conduct their business, provide for family life, send letters, travel throughout any region, thanks to the strong hand of Rome.

Instead of nibbling at the theological cheese laced with political arsenic set in the Pharisaical trap, Jesus impales his interrogators on the horns of a dilemma. Only two episodes previous, they had tried to impale *him* with a dilemmatic question about his authority. Now it was his turn to nick them: "Whose image? Whose inscription?" Touché!

From the pocket of his pin-striped silk suit, a Pharisee fished up a Roman coin. The image would be that of Tiberius, the reigning Emperor (And all the emperors called themselves Caesar. As did the Russians call themselves Tzar. And the Germans Kaiser—both titles derivatives of Caesar. What arrogance, these Russian and German tinpots, to make themselves in the image of a Roman Caesar!) And the inscription probably read, "Tiberius Caesar, divine Augustus, son of Augustus, pontifex maximus"— (high priest of the Roman nation).

"Give to Caesar Caesar's; give to God God's," Jesus said. "And they [the Pharisees and Herodians] were amazed at him" (17).

So what do we have here: mere repartee, adroit verbal sparring? Was it to be a fifty-fifty split? A division of temporal and spiritual kingdoms—until Christ's kingdom comes—or Constantine's, with the state swallowing the church, or Orthodox Russia, with the church swallowing the state? Not at all!

Once the simple equations and child-like rhymes of my youth satisfied; "pray, pay, obey," my old church fathers stated as the Christian's appropriate relationship to the state. But this spiritualizing notion of "a Jesus whose only concern about politics was to clarify that he was not concerned about politics" (John Howard Yoder), no longer satisfied me after a six-year sojourn in other cultural and religious milieus and into the Vietnam era.

The demands of Caesar—whether Roman, German, Russian, or American—dared to compete with God's. Something needed to be disentangled: What is Caesar's? What is God's? They were not conveniently on different levels, different agendas, different agents to which I could mindlessly bow both knees to both. "They are," as Yoder says in *The Politics of Jesus*, "in the same arena." His use of that word *arena* implies the fight of two powers for my allegiance, for my soul.

Could I really tell Christians—black and white—of South African apartheid, that ingeniously evil political system based on race, to obey its authors and henchmen? Could my pacifist conscience, founded on 500 years of Anabaptist belief, go on paying my federal income tax, more than half of which Uncle Sam uses to grease his military machines against Vietnamese: B-1 bombers at 250 million dollars each; Triton nuclear subs at nearly a billion a piece? Could I even pray for the toppling of a Nixon? Could I maintain my moral independence—God is sovereign, not Caesar, not Hitler, not Hussein, not Clinton, not Bush? These are matters contemporary Christians need to disentangle. One need not leave the Jesus times to find examples of people of faith clashing with Caesars, sorting out for those bone-heads what was God's.

Josephus, that ancient historian, tells in his *Antiquities* of how Pilate under cover of night introduced effigies of Caesar into Jerusalem. These hated images of a pagan god in their Holy City drove the Jews to a six-day siege of the imperial castle. Calling his troops to surround the protesters, Pilate threatened them with death. "But they threw themselves upon the ground and laid their necks bare and said they would take their death very willingly." Pilate, deeply moved by the Jews "to keep their laws inviolable," commanded the images to be removed.

Later, the Jews had a showdown with Gaius Caligula. The first Caesar to demand formal worship of himself installed a statue of himself in the temple at Jerusalem. The response was a general strike, fields left untilled in the sowing season, thousands protesting at Roman royal residencies. Petulant and snarling, old corrupt Caligula gave in and the sacrilegious statue was removed.

I must note, too, my own Virginia Mennonites during the Civil War. As almost nowhere else, to keep inviolable their peace convictions, they bore the brunt of their quiet noncooperation and civil disobedience to the Confederate military officers. As must every generation, they dared to remind the worshipers of Robert E. Lee, as did the ancient Jews to Caesar, how little was his.

Denying Death
Marriage at the Resurrection

The Sadducees, who say there is no resurrection, came to Jesus with a question. A woman married seven brothers; all died and left her child-less. "At the resurrection whose wife will she be?" Jesus replied, "When the dead rise, they will not marry. And about the dead rising—God said to Moses, 'I am the God of Abraham, Isaac and Jacob.' He is not the God of the dead, but of the living."—Mark 12:18-27

DEATH, RESURRECTION, MARRIAGE! Shelves sag with books on each topic. Might I delude myself with notions of any fresh musings on these subjects? The mind is a dragonfly, darting, skimming, from topic to topic. I should drum these wealthy, politically con-nected Sadducees for their old joke, as tiresome as a third-grader discovering riddles. Recite the old African tribal version of Moses' ancient levirate marriage laws (Deut. 24:5-10) as lived by the cook in a Tanzanian boys' school where I once taught.

I should note how all peoples make a heaven in the image of their earthly wishes: the desert Muhammad with his paradise of watered gardens and soft-eyed damsels; the North American na-tive with his happy hunting grounds; the frat brother at State U with his dream of an eternal beach with a beer and a broad. I should applaud Jesus' sly verbal riposte: since God is God of the living (Jesus then names as an example a dead trio: Abraham,

Isaac, and Jacob—knighting them with eternal life), implied is this: Some of you who are alive are dead to God!

Or admit to the impossibility of imagining my own death, to the horror of discontinuity, to heart's hunger for an afterlife. Recite the Scripture for consolation: "I know that my Redeemer lives, and that he will stand upon the earth. And in my flesh I will see God" (Job 19:25, 26). And "If in this life only we have hope in Christ, we are of all men most miserable" (1 Cor. 15:19). Listen again to Handel's choral arrangement for "The Messiah," a somber and exultant sliver: "Since by man came death, by man came also the resurrection of the dead. For as in Adam all die, even so in Christ shall all be made alive" (1 Cor. 15:21, 22).

But it's all that dying of those seven husbands which got me to thinking about death and pulling from the shelf to spot-read again in Ernest Becker's book, *The Denial of Death*. Drawing from Freud, Otto Rank, and Kierkegaard, Becker argues that while all peoples have feared death, only the modern have attempted to repress the knowledge of their own mortality. This is the source of much of our behavior and the root of our anxiety. Brilliant, brave, an electrifying read. For years I inflicted on lit students quotations from Becker; how valuable is his synthesis of modern psychological and philosophical thought in teaching Conrad, Mann, Woolf, Hemingway, and a dozen more. Any of the quotations from the following jumble show Becker's insight:

- "Man is literally split in two: he has an awareness of his own splendid uniqueness in that he sticks out of nature with a towering majesty—yet, he goes back into the ground a few feet in order blindly and dumbly to rot and disappear forever. It is a terrifying dilemma to be in and to have to live with" (26).
- "This is the terror: to have emerged from nothing, to have a name, consciousness of self, deep inner feelings, an excruciating inner yearning for life and self-expression— and with all this yet to die. It seems like a hoax—what kind of deity would create such complex and fancy worm food?" (87).

- "As soon as a man lifts his nose from the ground and starts sniffing at eternal problems like life and death, the meaning of a rose or a star cluster—then he is in trouble. Most men spare themselves the trouble by keeping their minds on the small problems of their lives as mapped out by society. These are what Kierkegaard called the 'Philistines,' who 'tranquilize themselves with the trivial'" (178).
- "For Kierkegaard 'philistinism' was triviality, man lulled by the daily routines of his society, content with the satisfactions that it offers him: in today's world the car, the shopping center, the two-week summer vacation. 'Philistinism tranquilizes itself in the trivial'" (74).
- People—whether blue collar workers or sophisticated cybertechnicians—use sex, art, and human relationships as distractions to deny mortality. Modern people "sell their souls to consumer capitalism or consumer communism or replace their souls with psychology. Psychotherapy is such a growing vogue today because people want to know why they are unhappy in hedonism. . . . Unrepression has become the only religion after Freud" (268).
- "A person spends years coming into his own, developing his talent, his unique gifts, perfecting his discrimination, broadening and sharpening his appetite, becoming mature, seasoned—taking sixty years of incredible suffering and effort to make such an individual, then he is good only for dying" (89).
- I conclude with a favorite passage, used as a warning shot across the bow of the budding hedonists in my classes! "Beyond a given point man is not helped by more 'knowing,' but only living and doing in a partly self-forgetful way (transcending the ego). As Goethe put it, we must plunge into experience and then reflect on the meaning of it. All reflection and no plunging drives us mad; all plunging and no reflection, and we are brutes" (199).

So end my reflections on living and dying, using one whose voice, admittedly, whispers to the dark side of my musings.

Love: Four or More
The Greatest
Commandment

A teacher of the law asked Jesus, "Which is the greatest command-
ment?" Jesus said, "Love the Lord. Love your neighbor." The lawyer
replied, "Love is more important than all burnt offerings and sacri-
fices." Jesus seeing that the man spoke wisely, said, "You are not far
from the kingdom of God." —Mark 12:28-34

MARK SAYS THAT JESUS WAS "DEBATING" with the Sadducees and
Herodians. Not a discussion, not a friendly spirited exchange,
but a debate: "a contention by words or arguments of opposing
views." Most recently on the matters of paying taxes, marrying
your brother's childless widow, rising from the dead. Now comes
a scribe, scorned by the other two sects who accommodate themselves with a bent law to toady to Roman occupiers. One is un-
sure of the motive behind the question: to learn, to debate, to
test, to have affirmed. But his question—"Which is the most important commandment?"—is of the kind every teacher relishes;
it provides a context for flashing wisdom dear to the teacher!

Jesus cited the Shema, the imperative of the Hebrew verb
"hear," the solemn recitation which opened each worship service, "Hear, O Israel: The Lord our God, the Lord is one. Love
the Lord your God with all your heart and with all your soul and
with all your strength" (Deut. 6:4). This Jewish confession is not

unlike the Christian creed which begins with *Credo,* Latin for "I believe." Surely the declamation "Allah is one God," which Muhammad would have heard often, mirrors the Jewish one.

But how does one "love God?" By word and by deed, yes. But severe rebuke awaited one who relied on "burnt offerings and sacrifices" as an expression of love. "I desire mercy, not sacrifice, and acknowledgment of God rather than burnt offerings" (Hos. 6:6). "Does the Lord delight in burnt offerings and sacrifices as much as in obeying the voice of the Lord? To obey is better than sacrifice" (1 Sam. 15:22). Sacrifices are meaningless without a heart which loves. Still, that is an abstraction.

One risks pride to declare in public assembly, "I love God!" A turn to the Psalter for instruction yields a surprise. How few, few, few are the poets' direct statements of affection to God. "I love you, O Lord, my strength" (18:1). "I love the Lord. . ." (116:1). And that's about it! But there are hundreds and hundreds of expressions of thanks for God's love toward the poet and his people, an utterance summed up centuries later by John: "Herein is love: not that we loved God, but that he loved us, and sent his Son as an atoning sacrifice for our sins" (1 John 4:10). There are lots of "O how I love thy Law!"

In one's private chamber and in one's car driving to work, one might exclaim in abandonment, "I love you, Lord." Otherwise to say it consciously, publicly, borders on spiritual exhibitionism—or so it strikes me. And I am struck mute when in a small group someone starts singing the religious ditty, "Jesus, I appreciate you. . . ." Appreciate? Like those old college courses which taught art and music appreciation!

"Love your neighbor." For the other half of the most important commandment, Jesus quoted from Leviticus. "Do not seek revenge or bear a grudge against one of your people, but love your neighbor as yourself" (19:18). It doesn't help to play dumb or wax philosophical or employ specious casuistry by asking, "Who is my neighbor?" Neighborliness, Jesus established, is one person showing mercy on another in need, even if that man is fool enough to bring ruin on himself.

Still, what is the character, quality, intensity, of this love toward such a fellow? It's easy enough to join Elizabeth Barrett Browning and say to one's lover, spouse, or child, "Let me count the ways I love thee." It's also easy to recite St. Paul's prescriptive recipe for love—both what love isn't and what love is. And one feels virtuous to instruct the wealthy paying up beyond a tithe with a reminder: charity is no substitute for equity. Smart, too, to note the "Four Loves" of C. S. Lewis: *storge* (affection), *philia* (friendship), *eros* (sexual love), and *agape* (divine gift-love).

Love is such a muddle of mixed emotions springing from mixed motives. In any one love experience, if one can cool down enough, have analytical skill sufficient, one finds traces of eros, agape, and narcissism—inexplicably simultaneous, inextricably enmeshed. Love is messy! Love needs nurturing and mopping up after!

Still, there is the matter of distinguishing love as a private moral ethic from the use of love as an institutional policy, even for an alleged Christian institution. For the latter, I come down on the side of E. M. Forster. In a 1941 essay entitled "Tolerance," he writes, "The idea that nations should love one another, or that business concerns or marketing boards should love one another, or that a man in Portugal should love a man in Peru of whom he has never heard—it is absurd, unreal, dangerous. It leads us into perilous and vague sentimentalism. The fact is we can only love what we know personally. And we cannot know much (or many)." He goes on to admit that "tolerance" is a very dull virtue, but argues very convincingly, it seems to me, that tolerance "carries on when love gives out."

I love my wife. I love my children and grandchildren. I love reading. I loved teaching. I loved students—well, some of them. I love violin concerti. I love May and October. I love broiled salmon and lime sorbet. I love retirement. And in my secret closet I say: "I love you, Lord."

Delight
Whose Son Is the Christ?

While Jesus was teaching in the temple courts, he asked, "How is it that the teachers of the law say that the Christ is the son of David? . . ." The crowd listened with delight. Jesus said, "Watch out for the teachers of the law. They like the best seats in the synagogue and the places of honor." —Mark 12:35-40

IT WOULD TAKE A MEDITERRANEAN MIND, a rabbinical hair-splitter, a Jesuit casuist, to answer Jesus' question! Someone steeped in the allusion and metaphor of Davidic psalms and the genealogies of the patriarchs—the who begat whom—would enjoy Jesus' riddle. Perhaps the crowd failed to align the verbal cubic he handed to the teachers of the law, but they listened with delight in Jesus' religious give-and-take. They could delight in an underdog who took a good if rare bite out of some ecclesiastic's seat of pants.

It would be fun to join Jesus and hurl verbal bricks at the religious aristocracy's slavering after dinner invitations to the most prestigious homes in Jerusalem's suburbs. To delight in his warnings against the professionally religious leaders, preachers, and professors at seminaries. To expose those schools of divinity where the name of God is taken often in vain but rarely in public confession and prayer. To write up my observation after attending a university church during grad school days. In that region of the U.S., the church for decades was the way out of cotton-field poverty. Get a call from the Lord, get into an endorsed seminary for a doctorate, then get a padded pulpit in The First Church of Town and preach to the comfortably pewed. "None of these preachers are going to knock the system that elevated and rewards them," a clear-eyed communicant explained to me.

But I need something to lighten the grim mood of these last days with Jesus. The religious aristocracy and the politically connected have grilled him; we've followed these bristling tete-a-tetes and feel exhausted. May we join the crowd in taking delight—not in Jesus' exchanges or his teachings? Rather, might we take a bit of playful delight in the word *delight* itself, before we turn back to widow's offerings, signs of the end of the age, and perfumed feet?

Delight: a high degree of pleasure or enjoyment; joy; rapture; something which gives great satisfaction. (Delight shares the same Latin root for the word *delectable*—delicious!) To charm; to enrapture.

The meaning and associated metaphors suggest a sensuality, a nearly physical passion for apprehending the spiritual. Because I am not solely a spiritual being, it becomes the old surprise of the spiritual having to manifest itself in the material!

Delight always strikes me as an inappropriate word to describe the Christian's posture or attitude toward the everlasting Supreme Being who redeems and judges. I suppose that reflects the "ungrace" of my dour childhood church and its distrust of all sensate experiences of delight. Yet there's the word, all through Scripture. In the Old Testament one expects to find delight among such sensuous books as the Song of Solomon. But the word is scattered lightly throughout the Psalms, the Proverbs, and Isaiah. Examples:

"Blessed is the man whose delight is in the law of the Lord" (Psalm 1:2). "Delight yourself in the Lord" (37:4). "I will go to God, who is my delight" (43:4). "Here is my servant . . . in whom I delight" (Isa. 42:1). "I delight greatly in the Lord" (41:10). Etc., etc., etc.! The New Testament too delights in God, in Christ, "in weaknesses, for Christ's sake!"

But I rarely can say the word delight and not think of a clutch of essays I first taught more than forty years ago. J. B. Priestley, an Englishman at home on both sides of the Atlantic, entitled one of his books *Delight*. This pocket-size collection of essays, some quite short, mere sketches, touches on the many topics of "the glorious trivia of living."

In "Cooking Picnics" (British for what Americans call "a cookout" or a "picnic" or a "barbecue"), Priestly writes of super-intending such events in that damp climate of his. Fried potatoes and sausages (and I shouldn't be surprised at all, from my experience with British cooking in East Africa, to find boiled cabbages—as they so properly insist on the plural for that bland vegetable—and a wrinkled Yorkshire pudding, at these cookouts) are a must. With every sinus smoke-wrecked, choking, and blasting away at children (I am surprised to find they take the kids on cookouts; thought they'd be locked away in their boarding schools!), and the fried chips gone rather soggy, "Somewhere there has been delight like a crumb of gold."

In "No School Report" J. B. as father confesses to "one secret little source of delight." Nobody now is sending home from school a report card on him. "What a nightmare it would be if again our personality were put through this mincing machine" (British for "meat grinder"). He imagines how all his teachers would note their displeasure with him: self-indulgent, lazy, vain, touchy, and bodily soft and saggy. "But it can't happen, not this side of the grave. I am knee-deep in the soggy world of graying hair and rotting teeth, of monstrous taxes and overdrafts, of vanishing friends and fading sight; but at least, I can tell myself delightedly, nobody is writing a school report upon me."

After delighting briefly in J. B. Priestly's take on middle-age life, we rejoin "the large crowd which listened to Jesus." Because we know the events of the coming week, a shadow falls over their delight in him. The shadow of the cross.

Two Coppers
The Widow's Offering

Jesus sat watching the crowds putting their money into the temple trea-sury. Rich people threw in large amounts. But a poor widow put in two very small copper coins. Jesus said to his disciples, "This poor widow, out of her poverty, put in everything—all she had to live on."
—Mark 12:41-44

LET US NOW SALUTE A GOOD, NAMELESS woman who offered every-thing she had to live on, part one (two comes later).

I hope this story of a nameless poor widow is true, coming as it does on the heels of Jesus' warning to the temple crowds: Watch those law teachers; they devour widows' houses! Set cheek-to-jowl the anecdote might illustrate Jesus' warning. Even if the two incidents did not occur in immediate chronology, I salute Mark's craftsmanship as writer to so arrange the text for heightened dramatic effect.

In that she's a widow (I'll accept what's reported of Jesus' knowledge of her marital status) perhaps she was one of the reg-ulars in Martha's kitchen at Bethany, where he spent some of his nights during his last, week-long visit to Jerusalem. I place her in the Women's Court. Again poring over the floor plan of the tem-ple, I find near the Gate Beautiful, between the Women's Court and Solomon's Porticoes, a clutch of collection boxes where of-ferings could be given for temple expenses.

Mark's verb to describe the action of the rich giving their offerings attracts one's attention. "Many rich people *threw* in large
amounts." The poor woman "put" in her two coppers. Out of
their great wealth the rich pitched in without the pain of sacrifice; they could hurry out to the handy ATM at the corner of
Goldman and Sachs for another thirty shekels of silver. The
widow stood before the trumpet-shaped offering receptacles,
paused, weighed her decision, then, generically, yet reverentially,
"put" in two coppers, each worth about one-sixteenth of a
penny—"all she had to live on."

By Jesus calling his disciples' attention to her sacrificial act of
devotion to God and her trust in his providence, the thin tinkle
of her coins was described repeatedly by some few of the twelve,
until Mark recorded the event. Now the clink of two coppers are
heard around the world. Having written that, I remember a
drama critic's remark about Nora Helmer's last act in Ibsen's *A
Doll's House*: "That slammed door reverberated across the roof of
the world." Nora's decision not to be her husband's childish play-
thing, abandoning her marriage to Torvald and her children,
shocked conventional middle-class sensitivities of nineteenth-
century Europe. It might just be the residue of the male chauvin-
ist pig in me, but I prefer the sound of two coppers falling to that
of "the reverberation of a heavy door closing."

In any event, this poor widow is memorialized for her sacrificial giving out of her poverty. No city library or university com-
mons or chapel to our Lady's Perpetual Poverty will be named for
her—we do not know her name, only her act. Unfortunately, too
many women are nameless in the records of Western civilization
and history. Even in genealogies. My own is an example; the
name of the woman who married the male progenitor of my
clan, who arrived in Philadelphia spring 1715, is not recorded in
the *Family Record of Preacher Benjamin Eby*. Here it is a lovely
and paradoxical thing; Jesus gave to history a lesson on the nature of generosity: a nameless poor widow gave two coppers.

The Christian and his money should raise the matter of
stewardship and tithing. The latter is often battered as a legalism

from which living in Christ has freed us. The former—the stewardship of all our resources—seems an alien, if not intrusive, notion to many Western Christians. I remember once broaching the topic of tithing with a single colleague, not to discipline, only to query. "I give nothing—the pathetic salary this church-institution pays me!"

My first noble attempts at tithing met with nearly the same results. A family of five, those first years of teaching, fresh back from a six-year stint of volunteering in Africa, without a stick of furniture—we often had to eat much of the tithe. Ate it with gladness! The Christmas gift for the eight-month-old child was a stack of old *Washington Post* newspapers. Her great joy was to crinkle newsprint. With ink-blackened hands, she looked up Christmas-radiant; she could not believe her luck!

One day that second year, the phone rang. A wealthy university professional, who still wants to be among nameless women, called to say she heard we were looking to buy a house. She had $20,000 available for a loan—a handsome amount in the early 1970s toward the purchase of a modest home. But why us? I did not ask. Yet her word-offering was as generous as her money-offering, words a young prof needed to hear. "You're the kind of people I believe in," she said.

The daily reminder of African poverty is no longer with us. Yet the memory is refreshed with stories from my wife's three-week visit a few years ago to the East African countries of her birth and childhood. Against the stories and memories, the wealth of European and North American countries is staggering. The private wealth of a handful of these northern residents is greater than the national budgets of at least three dozen countries south of the equator. In a little more than a decade, the gap between leading U.S. CEOs' incomes and their janitors' jumped from 30 times to 440 times. If the nameless woman leading a mop gets $20,000 (below poverty level for a family of four), the chief executive officer gets $8,800,000. Christ of the penniless widow, have mercy upon us!

·······················

Doom Approaches
The End of the Age,
the Hour Unknown

Jesus said, "You will hear of wars and rumors of wars . . . earthquakes and famines. Be on your guard; on account of me you'll be arrested. . . . The sun will be darkened, and stars will fall from the sky. At that time men will see the Son of man coming in clouds. When you see these things, you'll know the end is near. But no one knows the day or the hour, only the Father." —Mark 13:1-37

THIS FANTASTIC CHAPTER IN MARK reads like a pastiche from the prophets Amos, Joel, and Isaiah. Colored by the kaleidoscopic visions of the young Daniel in exile in Babylon and of the elderly John in exile on the Isle of Patmos. Perhaps best not to be taken literally, these impressionistic pictures of the Parousia, an apocalyptic unveiling about the last days of human history, had been with the Jewish people for centuries. According to Mark, Jesus touches on the following:

Things to come; the day of the Lord; prophecies of destruction; warnings of persecutions; warnings of last day dangers; warnings of false second comings; the necessity to be on watch; Jerusalem's destruction; its residents persecuted; the abomination of desolation; heresies of the last days—ending with prophecies about his own second coming. "Be watchful; be wakeful; be praying!"

The book of John's "Revelation" has stirred the imaginations of Christians from the time of its canonization. It's a mysterious mix of cosmic drama: four horsemen of the apocalypse; seven seals (a wax wafer, not a sea animal!); a beast with the mark of 666; the Whore of Babylon; the antichrist—and such prophetic utterances as that Jews will return to their Holy Land, a thousand-year reign of Christ on the earth, the Battle of Armageddon, a promise of a new heaven and a new earth.

Not surprisingly, this book fired the imaginations of dreamers, prophets, utopians. Martin Luther identified the papacy as the antichrist. The Puritans settling in Massachusetts imagined their theocratic colony a New Jerusalem. Apparitions of the Virgin Mary appeared at Lourdes. Hal Lindsey sold 30 million copies of *The Late Great Planet Earth*. My own sweet father-in-law, who spent a life-time planting churches in East Africa, steeped in the interpretations of Daniel's visions, expected to be living when Christ returned. When he died, I tried saluting his life in Africa, his love for Jesus, his longing for the Grand Finale, by writing a poem. A few lines read—

> Still, ever the watchman of the night for the
> last dawn, he mounted the stairs, alone.
> There, said from memory, Blood-soaked Hebrews,
> then fell from bed, dead. Parousia had come!
> A private feast of silent trumpets blared his day.
> No bloody moon lay over the land; the northern
> bear found toothless. No antichrist smeared
> abominations in places of desolation—just
> a private parousia: an inexplicable mystery,
> a divine joke? No, now he walks in the light;
> he knew how to repent. "*Utukufu*. Alleluia!"
> Praise for the Blood of the Lamb!

American-Africans, when still known as Negroes, gave us wonderful music and poetry which touch the judgment, the terror and the bliss, heaven and hell, the end times. One spiritual opens with, "In that great gittin'-up mornin'—we shall rise! Fare ye well! Fare ye well!"

Meanwhile in James Weldon Johnson's *God's Trombones*, the last of seven Negro sermons in verse, "The Judgment Day," speaks of when at time's end "With a wave of his hand God will blot out time,/And start the wheel of eternity." Then where will we sinners stand, James Weldon Johnson asks, "In that great day when God's a going to rain down fire?"

Contemporary writers call it "Waiting for Godot," and "I hear there's one hell of a good universe next door; let's go there and see!" The hymnbook of my youth was much less cavalier about the Transposition. Still we rarely sang No. 296, "The Day of Wrath." Words by a thirteenth-century Italian Catholic priest, music in a minor key, the hymn fit the gloomy mood of my soul, a tender responsive mirror to a God of damnation, to the terror of a Paradise Lost.

Here was a terrible God whom I would meet years later in the wild-haired images of William Blake. Once, when I could lead congregational music, I selected the hymn, most unfittingly on a soft summer evening full of fire flies and the smell of drying alfalfa hay.

> The day of wrath, that dreadful day
> When heav'n and earth shall pass away!
> What pow'r shall be the sinner's stay?
> How shall he meet that dreadful day?
> O on that day, that wrathful day,
> When man to judgment wakes from clay,
> Be thou, O Christ, the sinner's stay,
> Tho' heav'n and earth shall pass away.

Later, undergoing aesthetic refinement, I met in college choir Randall Thompson's *The Peaceable Kingdom*, a work commissioned by the Harvard Glee Club and the Radcliffe Choral Society, long after the Puritan divines preached hellfire and resident clerics made of hell a mother-in-law or an abusive childhood. I loved singing—howling, actually—"Their children also shall be dashed to pieces before their eyes. . . ." And "Howl Ye!" This fourth chorus I wanted to go on all afternoon, instead of only seventeen pages (already a fifth of the choral book), but that a cheat. Scored for a double chorus, the pages flipped by rapidly with a mere faint rustle to our youthful but earnest howling.

Perfume
Jesus Anointed at Bethany

While Jesus was in Bethany, reclining at the table in the home of
Simon the Leper, a woman came with a jar of very expensive perfume.
She broke the jar and poured the perfume on his head. "Why wasn't
this sold, the money given to the poor?" the disciples said. To which,
Jesus said, "Leave her alone. She has done a beautiful thing to me. The
poor you have with you always. . . . Wherever the gospel is preached
throughout the world, what she has done will also be told, in memory
of her." —Mark 14:1-11

LET US NOW SALUTE GOOD NAMELESS women who offered everything they had to live on, part two (one came earlier).

Nameless this woman was for Mark. But John seems to have
spoiled her anonymity by declaring the woman to be Mary, a
good Bible student but a slouch in her sister's kitchen. Martha
was hosting a dinner in honor of Jesus, according to John. She
was uneasy these days; something ominous hung in the
Jerusalem air. Food was a pleasant distraction: an appetizer of
grape paste on toasted, unleavened rye; a creme of tomato soup;
a brisket of lamb in rosemary and olive; rice pudding topped
with Cool Whip; tea; a local red wine; a wedge of goat Brie. But
she would have to keep an eye on Mary, sweet and devout but
flighty. With the twelve other men in the house, Mary was apt to
lose her head.

She did, just before dessert. Threw off her scarf, freed her hair, and stood fumbling with an alabaster jar. Then she whacked it against the frame of the reclining couch on which the men lay. Poured out a five-years' supply of perfume—"Evening in Mesopotamia"—on Jesus' feet. Cloyed the air with a rich, rich odor—a blend of nutmeg, rose, and ox musk. Filled the chamber. No one any longer could smell the dinner. Then Mary stooped, and flinging her hair across the front of her head, she knelt and wiped the Rabbi's feet. The twelve pulled in their feet in horror. Martha stood frozen in dumbstruck shock in the dining room doorway. It took the clatter of a maid-servant dropping a skillet in the kitchen to unthaw her.

I'm of two minds about whether this unnamed woman in Mark is actually Mary of John. Pouring perfume on a male guest's feet seems just the thing Mary would do. She'd been around Jesus' feet before—sitting there as he taught about Life in his kingdom. Perhaps she admired his strong dark feet. That here they were again, exposed, rather carried her away. On the other hand, the act seems too intimate between common friends. One of them would burst out laughing, the other would turn to tickling. Perfuming the feet would have to be done by a woman strange to Jesus yet attracted by the magnetism of his message and character.

Something should be said sometime about Jesus as a highly eligible bachelor in his early thirties. May as well acknowledge it here. Surely Jesus attracted women, good and shady. But his easy manner among them suggests he was no prude. He was no Pharisee, meeting a woman in the market, lowering his eyes lest he lust over a bare brown limb, then running into a lampost, bloodying his nose for piety. Women were first of all human—made of the flesh he had entered into with his incarnation. Gender and social class and marital status did not matter.

With—let us keep this woman nameless—her anointing of Jesus, she performed a Jewish funeral ritual in advance of his death. Jesus elevated her extravagance to a holy moment ("She has done a beautiful thing"), annealed her abandonment in worship to the proclamation of his gospel ("Wherever the gospel is preached throughout the world, what she has done will also be told").

It's John again who names people. This time he pins the charge of grumbler about women and their extravagant use of perfume on Judas Iscariot. John also uses the occasion here to remind his readers about this: It was "Judas who was later to betray him." And only a breath later, "He did not say this because he [Judas] cared about the poor but because he was a thief; as keeper of the money bag, he used to help himself to what was put into it." I say: it's a good thing Judas didn't live to read this accusation. Those words would end with the saintly John in court on a charge of defamation of character.

I know little about perfume, except when I smell too much and my throat begins to freeze. And when I stroll through the department store and some painted doll at Jezebel's counter sprays me with a shot so strong it anesthetizes me. But once during my years in Somalia, a student invited me to his wedding, held in the colonnaded shade of the old Arab quarters of Mogadishu. At one point in the ceremony, at which no women, not even the bride, attended (from behind the shuttered windows of a three-floor apartment they looked down on the men and at appropriate times gave their ululating joy cries), servants sprinkled the guests with perfume from tall, slim, silver decanters. Lovely! An idea for my own wedding!

Years later in Paris on a professional visit with a male colleague, I decided to bear home the appropriate gifts to a wife: silk scarves, chocolates, perfume. In a large glass-walled perfume shop just across the street from the Louvre and its newly installed glass pyramids, I stood transfixed. The sales clerk wanted me to describe my wife: Bewitching? Dark? Playful? Tilting toward domesticity? The clerk wanted to find a fragrance to accompany her personality. Twelve years later the bottle de Capucci sits evaporating away in her drawer. I ate the chocolates (they made her queasy). I do not wear the silk scarves!

Bread and Wine
The Lord's Supper

So Jesus and his disciples prepared the Passover. While reclining at the table eating, Jesus took bread, gave thanks and broke it, and gave it to his disciples, saying, "Take it; this is my body." Then he took the cup, gave thanks and offered it to them. "This is my blood of the covenant, which is poured out for many." —Mark 14:12-26

ON HEARING THESE WORDS OF OUR LORD read at Holy Communion, rarely do I escape a memory of a grievous failure of mine in a classroom at the University of Virginia. Every Tuesday and Thursday morning that spring semester I drove over Afton Mountain from the Shenandoah Valley to Jefferson's "Academical Village" for a course in the Metaphysical Poets. A British-born Israeli citizen, Distinguished Visiting Professor of English, Eminent Scholar of Seventeenth Century British Literature, Mr. Ralston (in UVA's time-honored imitation of traditions at Cambridge and Oxford, he, too, was only Mister) both chilled and warmed me. His pedagogical method terrorized the class—well, at least this less-than-scholarly student; his daily breaking open of Donne, Herbert, Marvel—well, "I felt my soul strangely stirred."

Following two weeks of brilliant lectures on seventeenth century England—government, religion, culture, world exploration, inventions and discoveries, court and drawing room protocol—he assigned daily four or five poems on which we were to give oral explications when he called on us the next period. Rarely did we cover more than two poems in the ninety minutes. Nor did we know which of us nine students would be favored by his cool invitation to speak.

Ralston, in thick cardigans, tweedy jackets, and suede shoes, would enter the classroom, greet us civilly, and sit down at the teacher's desk. Then without preliminary light chatter about the weekend, he'd open his copy of the metaphysical poets, glance at a tally sheet, and call on one of us to begin the explication of a poem.

And thus one of us would attempt a word-by-word illumination of a three-hundred-year-old poem with its high-flown and extravagant wit and the embrace of its era's cosmography. Our voices often raised at the ends of sentences, in limp, imploring interrogative query: Am I saying anything correctly? Ralston would never comment, not so much as a murmur of assent. With his refined manners, he would not interrupt a budding scholar at his labor.

So on we'd plow, laying open a ragged ditch through a Donne conceit or a Herbert incongruity. Plowing turned to stumbling and floundering. When finally, inevitably, we fell on our faces, exhausted over a mangled field, Mr. Ralston would thank us, stand up, and begin the restoration of grace and wit that enshrouded the poem.

The prof handled the religious poems—half of Donne, nearly the whole of Herbert, a smattering of Marvel—with reverence, never scorning their Christian theological underpinnings or allusions, backgrounding for minutes some bit of orthodoxy based on St. Paul, revealing Christ the Lamb, Christ the Tiger. I saw in him a model of all that I tried to be in my own university classroom. One who had integrated faith and learning. Surely this man was a believer and bore witness in the classroom daily with the manner of his scholarly handling of poetry, sacred and risque. Then one day it all blew apart.

A middle-aged woman, like me, always sat against a low window. With her back to the light, she appeared as a dark silhouette, lumpish in her heavy parka. Usually quiet, that day she exploded. I can no longer recall the poem under dissection—probably something like these lines from Donne's "The Agonie":

> Love is that liquour sweet and most divine,
> Which my God feels as blood; but I, as wine.

"All this blood, blood, blood," she exploded, "this Christian drinking of Jesus' blood—it's religious cannibalism! It's repulsive to me—a Jew! Can anyone help me to respond intellectually if not emotionally to these poems?" She looked up at Mr. Ralston.

He took one light step backwards from her verbal blast, raised his two hands palms outward, and gave an elegant little shrug. "Don't look to me," he said. "I'm an agnostic!"

I was shocked! This man who broke open the word daily with such sympathy to Christian symbols and theology was better than a dozen preachers I'd sat under for forty years! How could this be? But just then I was spared the exploration of that thought. He glanced about the class, his gaze passing over me—my prayer answered before uttered. I was not a young, frightened, newborn to the faith, but I was not good at oral repartee, even for a holy witness. I prayed: let this cup pass by me. And it did. Ralston called on the only other male. "Mr. Jones, aren't you a Lutheran priest?" The poor youth fumbled, and so the moment passed into oblivion.

Except for me. Later a sense of shame darkened my spirit. I could have publicly joined my Jewish classmate's repulsion. Transubstantiation also galls me, theologically and aesthetically. On the communion table in my church are carved four simple words that say it all: "In Remembrance of Me." Only that, we eat bread and drink wine in memory of our Lord's death, using symbols the Lord himself introduced. Surely my classmate, practicing or atheist, could appreciate the universal appropriateness of bread and wine. Eaten in silence, the Eucharist is ritual without language.

Friends and Friendship
Jesus Predicts
Peter's Denial

*"You will all fall away," Jesus told his disciples when they went out to
the Mount of Olives. Peter declared, "I will not." Jesus answered,
"Tonight, before the rooster crows twice you will disown me three
times." But Peter insisted emphatically, "I will never disown you." And
all the others said the same. —Mark 14:27-31*

WE ALL NEED FRIENDS, SEVERAL GOOD lifetime friends, but only a
few intimate friends. What a surprise for the young married couple to discover that their lover, now spouse, "their significant
other," in psychological jargon, does not fully meet their needs
for friendship, affection, love. How immature of them to impose
such a weight on one person. How mature when they learn to
relax and to mend old severed friendships, particularly of their
own gender.

Peter's declaration of "always being there" for Jesus raises a
query into the need and nature of friendship, particularly among
males. As here with Jesus and the twelve, with the intimate three,
and with Peter's public expressions of the steadfastness of his
friendship for Jesus.

Literature is full of poetry, essay, and story about friendship—and I deliberately use this word in my musings on this

Markian passage, rather than the word "love" with its layered meanings.

One can start with lines from Emerson's "Friendship," picking the essay up anywhere, because of its rambling construction. One doesn't find here the polished phrases of Francis Bacon, often considered the first essayist in English literature. Rather, here is the loose personal essay which enjoys the writer's voice and whim.

"A friend is a person with whom I may be sincere. Before him I may think aloud," Emerson writes. "I am arrived at last in the presence of a man so real and equal that I may drop even those undermost garments of dissimulation, courtesy, and second thought. . . . Sincerity is the luxury allowed. . . . A friend may well be reckoned the masterpiece of nature."

Fiction, too, explores the quality of friendship. One fine example reveals the nature of friendship between men and brothers: Conrad's *The Lagoon.* Courtesies now aside, the evening late, Arsat, of the Polynesian Islands, risks speaking of love (his older brother dead, his wife dying) to his old white friend: "Where can we lay down the heaviness of our trouble but in a friend's heart?" He relates how earlier he had confessed to his brother his love for a woman forbidden to him because of her service to royalty; how his brother agreed to help them elope; how this brother died in assisting him to slip away with the woman. This simple young man knew this great wisdom: "There's no worse enemy and no better friend than a brother, for one brother knows another, and in perfect knowledge is strength for good or evil. I loved my brother."

But the Christian soon wants something more from an intimate friendship. About such longing, Englishman Alan Jones writes in an essay on Christian friendship. "I become less interested in the popular demand for self-affirmation than in the need for the development of a strenuous honesty about myself: a self who can stand being scrutinized because he knows he is loved. The friends I value most are those who love me unreservedly but with discrimination. They are willing to scrutinize me. . . . I need someone who penetrates my senseless ceaseless chatter and see the terrific thing there really is in me" (26).

And another quotation from Jones: "A spiritual friend is one who both stimulates the imagination and also helps me gain a critical distance from the main currents and events of my life so that I can take a fresh look at where I am and where I am going."

Jones asks for that quality of friendship which feels like a warm shower bath, such as memorialized between the men David and Jonathan. On death of the one, the other cries, "You were very dear to me. Your love for me was wonderful" (29).

The continuing friendships of former students surprises me. I had thought such associations would not survive the classroom and the professor's office. I came to learn that the best were reciprocal. I was ministered to by even the ones who came looking for help. Their frank questions, their young hopes, kept waking me up, kept refreshing me in the faith, in a manner I could not have expected.

Of course not only I but others too have experienced such bonding. One former student, now in his forties, wrote to his old prof, between whom had grown up a twenty-year friendship. "Having been caught up in a bit of your history, having subsequently explored it and a bit of my own via our many letters, I find our souls have mingled. And the mingling of souls makes for good history. The offering of yourself, the witness of generosity, the making possible of commingling—teacher with student, friend with friend, soul with soul. That's what we most want to do, I believe: make good history together."

Peter went on, of course, to make good history based on his three-year friendship with his teacher Jesus. A friendship which under a terrible tender scrutiny by his teacher Peter must confess "love" three times to remove three denials. Until hurt, he whispered, "Lord, you know all things; you know that I love you."

Olive Press
Gethsemane

They went to a place called Gethsemane, and Jesus said to his disciples, "Sit here while I pray." He took Peter, James and John along with him, and he began to be deeply distressed and troubled. "My soul is overwhelmed with sorrow to the point of death," he said to them. Going alone further he prayed, "Take this cup from me." Three times he returned to his disciples to find them sleeping. Then he said, "Enough! The hour has come." —Mark 14:32-42

FROM THE MOUNT OF OLIVES, JESUS and the eleven (Judas now off on his mission to betray) walked a little further in full Paschal moonlight to the Olive Press (Gethsemane). I remember my morning walk in the Garden of Gethsemane in full Mediterranean sunlight. The olive grove—owned by the Armenian, Greek, and Russian churches—was meticulously cared for by the Franciscans of the Roman Catholic church. I did not care for the Russian Orthodox church shouldering itself into a holy place; its organically shaped architecture of onion domes seemed incongruous in an olive garden. Fortunately, one could turn one's back on the church and meditate on the lovely ancient olive trees—some estimated to be three thousand years old. Later, in a small shop, since visitors were forbidden to pick up even one dropped olive leaf on the gravel path, I bought a dried one pressed protectively between a small souvenir sheet.

How wonderfully fitting is this place for the Visitor and his prayer. *Press*. A dozen images associated with press rise in the mind, beyond that simple machine to extract liquid from olives, grapes, apples. The press of a crowd; the defensive crowding on the basketball court; the action of weight lifting; the collective ethos of news reporters and broadcasters, their machines and products. And not only actions, but attitudes associated with press: squeeze, harass, afflict, exert, contend. Press—pressure. Physical and psychological. At this Olive Press, Jesus experienced the full range of "press"—against his body, against his soul.

"My soul is overwhelmed with sorrow to the point of death," Jesus said to his disciples. He "began to be deeply distressed and troubled." Pressed, he turned to his trio of intimate friends to speak aloud, for the first time, the full terror of his mission. But they were dulled with fighting sleep.

This is a terrible moment! I am wrenched with grief. We all want someone near us in time of trouble. Not for the distraction of chatter, nor even the sincere attempts at verbally sharing grief. Someone who "will *listen* actively and purposefully, responding with . . . the personal vulnerability of his own trembling self," as Sheldon Kopp puts it in *If You Meet the Buddha on the Road, Kill Him*. While he addresses guru-therapists, it is applicable to all intimate friendships. We are to offer ourselves. This involves the "cultivation of a naked awareness, remembering all the time that we are really going to die, that we each suffer from the same terminal disease."

What deeply troubled Jesus' soul was not only his knowledge of how the Romans executed criminals. The powers of darkness assailed him. The torments of doubt were loosed upon him. Could it be that he didn't understand fully his own mission? What keeping faith with a sense of his calling might fully entail? Had the overwhelming sorrow more to do with a psychological terror: had he just possibly deluded himself by his own words and actions—that they were not of the Father? Had he already some premonition of a Father's abandonment of his son, either deliberately or because he himself is powerless?

Here, now at the end of his ministry, Jesus is alone, tempted as he once was at the beginning. Then, hungry, he battled Lucifer; here he wrestles with the very God, his own Father. On both occasions the temptations offer easy solutions: then, make miraculous stone-bread, worship the False Power; here, step aside from this rendezvous with death, don't drink the cup. This is the Man-Jesus earning the full measure of what it means to be man. Like us, he too prays earnestly for escape from the coming terror. So we see him as one of us, not the serene God-Jesus sailing "to the skies on rosy beds of ease."

I remember Luke writes that "angels ministered to him." But that aside, doesn't Jesus' prayer here in Gethsemane show that anxiety is also part of God's will for our human destiny? C. S. Lewis in *Letters to Malcolm: Chiefly on Prayer* sums up the Gethsemane scene is this manner. "Does not every movement in the Passion write large some common element in the sufferings of *our human race*? First, the prayer of anguish; not granted. Then He turns to His friends. They are asleep, as ours, or we, are so often, or busy, or away, or preoccupied. Then he faces the Church; it condemns Him. . . . Then, nothing left but God. And God, God's last words are 'Why hast thou forsaken me?'" (43).

"Enough!" Jesus said, before waking his disciples and turning toward the bobbing torches of Judas and the armed crowd. What did he mean by that one word: *enough*? Sufficient, fully, quite, no more, received in full, settled? How did he say it? Triumphantly, or with quiet resignation? Does it foreshadow one of his last seven words from the cross—"It is finished"? However, whatever—"Enough!" gathers up all the layers of nuances about his own position, his exhausted disciples, and the chief priests and scribes, who'd been playing their cat-and-mouse games with him that last week.

The Kiss
Jesus Arrested

Judas appeared with a crowd armed with swords and clubs, sent from the chief priests, the scribes and the elders. Going at once to Jesus, Judas kissed him. The men seized Jesus and arrested him. "Am I leading a rebellion, that you come armed? Every day I was in the temple courts and you didn't arrest me." Everyone deserted Jesus and fled. A young man when seized fled naked. —Mark 14:43-50

THE SETTING FOR THIS EPISODE IS THE stuff of sentimental Christian fiction and amateur sanctuary plays: midnight in a garden, the glint of torch-flares among olive trees, an armed mob, a kiss, a naked young man running away, a full moon suddenly clouded over, an innocent Rabbi seized like a guerrilla. So Mark's spare style should be noted again. Here, with a scene of high drama, his control of language is admirable, elegant, restrained. American poet Ezra Pound would say of Mark's style, as he did of Hemingway's, "Less is more." In that theory the more an emotion is suggested rather than stated, the more feeling, paradoxically, is evoked. Mark's telling is powerful because it does not indulge in sentimentality, in an overflow of florid prose to render a passionate grief.

No staged production I've seen quite captures the treachery, grit and shame of Jesus' betrayal and arrest—not the Hollywood versions of a half dozen films, nor the more recent productions by televangelists. Even the Black Hills Passion Play, at Spearfish, South Dakota, seemed stagy and passionless. Part of their failure surely lies in the genius of Mark to wield with a mere 165 words a powerful scene which the imagination fleshes out in a brisk, intense drama no "outside" production can match.

My readings on this passage of Mark raises interest in two words: *kiss* and *rebellion*. The readers of New Testament Greek tell us that two different words are used here for our one English word kiss. Judas to the henchmen instructed, "The one I *kiss* is the man." Here Judas used *philein*, the kiss common to the Palestinian greeting of one man to another, as seen on our evening news, not only of Mediterranean peoples, but Russians, Italians, and South Americans. The kiss, too, was given by a student to his beloved Teacher. The next line of the text reads, "Going at once to Jesus, Judas said, 'Rabbi' and *kissed* him." Here Mark used *kataphilein*, the kiss of lovers given on the lips. This little prefix—*kata*—heightens the treachery of this betrayal. The prearranged sign is not just the common formal kiss of respectful greeting. Judas gave Jesus a lover's kiss. His deceit negates the truth of Proverbs 24:26: "An honest answer is like a kiss on the lips."

Briefly, about Jesus' use of the word *rebellion*. He chided the henchmen of the religious establishment sent to arrest him, "Am I leading a rebellion, that you come out with swords and clubs to capture me?" Other translations use "thief," and "bandit"—a leader of marauders, a guerrilla leader of a resistance-movement. Jesus' word (whatever he used in the original Aramaic) seems a deliberate ironic tease. He indeed led a movement against a religion shot through with hypocrisy, one supported by collaborators with pagan political oppressors. While no Bin Laden or Che Guevera—more in the flavor of Martin Luther or Mahatma Gandhi—Jesus and his gospel of the New Kingdom had social and political dimensions not short of a call for a bloodless revolt.

A modern bit of betrayal is played out in Graham Greene's novel, *The Power and the Glory*. This is a novel I reread every year in British Fiction class, a novel I embraced as a weapon to prick any placid Anabaptist student not believing in the sacramental efficacy of the Eucharist to an understanding of "grace." How did they understand that grace came to them, using St. Paul's words: "It is by grace you have been saved" (Eph. 2)?

In southern Mexico, during an anti-clerical purge by the local Marxist government, the last priest, a whisky priest, is on the run from a police lieutenant, an ideological fanatic. A poor, hideously ugly mestizo, a half-caste (half Spanish, half Indian) cannot resist the 700-peso reward offered for tipping off the police on the whereabouts of the priest. Early, the mestizo suspects the shabby lone traveler through his village to be that priest. Attaching himself like a leech, the mestizo one night in an abandoned hut says, "Father, hear my confession. You couldn't refuse a man in mortal sin." When the priest says nothing, the mestizo goes on carefully. "I won't betray you. I'm a Christian." At that, the priest's "conscience ceased to accuse him of uncharity. He knew. He was in the presence of Judas."

Later that same night, the priest attempts to give the slip to the mestizo. He thinks that "It was too easy to die for what was good or beautiful, for home or children, or a civilization—it needed a God to die for the half-hearted and corrupt. Christ had died for this man too. This was Judas sick and unsteady and scared in the dark. How could he pretend with his pride and lust and cowardice to be any more worthy of that death than the half-caste? This man intended to betray him for money which he needed, and he had betrayed God for what?—"

The priest, too, tastes Jesus' temptation. "Self-preservation lay across his brain like a horrifying obsession." Yet in prison he freely confesses to the prisoners, "I am a whisky priest." Then wonders "where the inevitable Judas was sitting now." But then, inexplicably, he was moved by "an irrational affection for the inhabitants of this prison. A phrase came to him: 'God so loved the world'. . . ."

Silence and Speech
Jesus Before the
Sanhedrin

They took Jesus to the Sanhedrin who looked for evidence against him so they could put him to death. Many testified falsely, but their testimonies did not agree. The high priest asked Jesus, "Aren't you going to answer?" But Jesus remained silent and gave no answer. Then the high priest asked, "Are you the Christ?" And Jesus said, "I am, and you'll see the Son of man sitting at the right hand of the Mighty One...." The high priest tore his clothes, and they all condemned him as worthy of death. —Mark 14:53-65

> *So ist mein Jesus nun gefangen*
> Behold, my Jesus is now taken.
> *Mond und Licht*
> Moon and stars
> *ist vor Schmerzen untergangen; ...*
> have in grief gone dark; ...
> *Sind Blitze, sind Donner in Wolken verschwunden?*
> Have lightning and thunder abandoned the heavens?
> *Eroffne den feurigen Abgrun, o Holle,*
> Open your fiery abyss, O hell,
> *zertrummre, verderbe, verschlinge, serchelle*
> destroy them, overwhelm them, devour and consume them

mit plotzlicher Wut
with a sudden rage—
den falschen Verater, das mordrische Blut!
the treacherous betrayer, the murderous blood!

These nights I have been listening to music fitting the days' readings and musings, music of death and dying: Mozart's "Requiem," Bach's "Mass in B Minor" and "The Passion According to St. Matthew"—the sorrowful music of soul to soul. And reading program notes and translations of texts. I read in Albert Schweitzer's notes, "Bach's B minor Mass was never performed in his lifetime." How could such sublime and tender music go unsung! Bach took liberties with the strict liturgical scheme, adding Lutheran expressions to a Catholic mass. "A Protestant would never have performed a Catholic mass, and the Catholic church would never have suffered the deviations from the set liturgy," Schweitzer notes. That was the mid-1770s. Today, much of the Christian church is ecumenical in its music. "The Mass in B Minor is Catholic and Protestant at the same time, and for all that, so enigmatic and unfathomably deep as the master's own religious mind." Palpable even for a simple Anabaptist.

Jesus stood before the Supreme Court of the Jews, before the semicircles of seventy-one members of the Sanhedrin: Sadducees, Pharisees, scribes, and respected elders. These intellectuals of theology and law made of justice a burlesque show of grotesque incongruity—their court couldn't even get false witnesses to agree!

Before such noise Jesus observed the wisdom, "There is a time to be silent." One does not need to honor charges that are hearsay, lies, distortions. Yet when asked directly, "Are you the Christ?" it was "a time to speak." One is amazed at the courage it took to affirm this query. Jesus knew his answer, "I am," would incriminate him. But he quickly claimed that other title, "The Son of man," a phrase borrowed from Daniel's vision. By it he owned his incarnation in human flesh, became the defenseless sufferer who in the end wins not by conquering and killing but by his own death at the hands of the powers before him.

The tenor in Bach's "Passion According to St. Matthew" (also quoted at the opening of this musing) sings in a recitative—

> Mein Jesus schweigt zu falschen Lugen stille, um uns damit zu zeigen
> My Jesus answers nothing to false witness, to show us
> *dass sein Erbarmens voller Wille vor uns zum Leiden sie geneigt,*
> that his will filled with mercy for us is bowed toward sorrow,
> *und dass wir in dergleichen Pein*
> and that when we are in similar pain
> *ihm sollen ahnlich sein, und in Verfolgung stille schweigen.*
> we should be like him, and in persecution remain silent.

One must not forget two men who sat in that Sanhedrin: Nicodemus, the Pharisee who had a tete-a-tete with Jesus by night and later brought 100 pounds of myrrh and aloes to prepare the body for burial; and Joseph of Arimathea, a wealthy secretive disciple of Jesus who personally sought permission of Pilate to bury Jesus' body, possibly in his own stone-hollowed tomb. But they could effect no stay against the inevitability of Jesus' death sought by their peers.

Like Helen Suzman in the South African Parliament for many years. A member of the Progressive Party, winning her seat from a white Johannesburg suburb, Houghton, she cast vote after vote against apartheid, that ingenuously evil system designed by the sons of Christ and Calvin. Often she voted along with only one or two other members, some of those few members of Alan Paton's Liberal Party. They could effect nothing against the white regime but remained a voice whispering in a politically immoral wilderness.

The Sanhedrin "looked for evidence against Jesus." To which Jesus said, "Why question me? Ask those who heard me" (John 18:21). A few among those who "heard" yet were not invited to bear witness at that trial include these:

- Simon Peter's mother-in-law;
- a leper;
- a paralytic dropped to Jesus through a roof;
- a stone mason with a shriveled hand;

- Legion, a devil-possessed man who lived among cave-tombs;
- Jairus, a synagogue ruler and his raised-from-the-dead daughter;
- a woman inflicted with a twelve-year bleeding;
- five thousand picnickers;
- a Syrophoenician woman and her possessed little daughter;
- four thousand picnickers;
- a rich young ruler;
- the sunset Galilean crowds in the Capernaum suburb of Bethsaida.

A Rooster Crows
Peter Disowns Jesus

Peter was in the courtyard of the high priest, warming himself. A servant girl looked closely at him. "You're with that Nazarene, Jesus," she said. A second and third time she said to Peter: surely you're one of those Galileans. Three times Peter denied it, taking an oath. "I don't know the man!" Immediately the rooster crowed the second time. Then Peter remembered the word Jesus had spoken to him. He went out and wept. —Mark 14:66-72

HERE IS A CAMEO PORTRAIT, A FINGERNAIL sketch, of a man's sin and remorse. Bone-weary from a sleepless night, exhausted with emotional outbursts leading to blood, bleary in the gray hours before dawn, Peter was provoked into a denial of Jesus by a cheeky snot. A servant girl in the high priest's mansion, she felt herself protected, could identify and lead in charging Peter as an accomplice to the criminal being tried in her master's house. Others standing by took up the accusation.

But before first cock crowed, Peter had time to review the night: sleepy, he dozed through Jesus' Gethsemane; slashing about with a borrowed sword he sliced off the ear of a servant to the high priest; half-heartedly he followed the crowd shoving his Teacher toward infamy; then, cursing and swearing, he declared, "I don't know the man."

What a man is Peter! At once audacious and devious. Having sliced up the high priest's servant, Peter might be forgiven for not pitching up at that house. Yet there he was, even if slouching through the early morning chill to warm himself at the enemy's fire. (Presumably none of the other twelve even slunk along—Judas was somewhere still in the olive garden, mulling over his money, nursing remorse, sliding irreparably toward a terminal blue funk.) But Peter was there, keeping his word—well, keeping at least half of it. Just hours previous he had declared, "Even if all fall away, I will not." That piece of his promise he kept. About the latter—"Even if I have to die with you, I will never disown you"—instantly memory of Jesus' words assault him with the rooster's second crow of announcing the false dawn. Flooded with remorse, Peter "broke down and wept." A cameo of denial and grief.

Seeing a big man shaken by tears is a terrible sight. Chest muscles heave in spasms, the face above the beard contorts in grief, at last the voice breaks out into an inconsolable howl. Here, a big man is broken open by the mere crowing of a proud cockerel somewhere in the High Priest's chicken coop.

How rightly Carmen Bernos de Gastold catches the pride with gentle irony the voice of the cock in her *Prayers from the Ark*. While confessing that it needs "some glitter and ostentation," twice it proudly reminds God, "I am Your servant. I make the sun rise."

One wishes for Peter a dawn's greeting by a bird other than that cock. Instead of his heart harrowed by a rooster crowing, Peter's "heart in hiding, stirred for a bird," as was Gerard Manley Hopkins on glimpsing the windhover. That Peter could have cried, "I caught this morning's minion, kingdom of daylight's dauphin, dapple-dawn drawn Falcon!" Caught the soaring updraft of that beauty and not the spiraling down to grief. That Peter could have found himself "stirred," not in shame by words that "fall, gall themselves," but by the "brute beauty and valour," by the "fire that breaks from thee (Christ). . . O my chevalier!"

Peter must have told others, perhaps often, about his night's betrayal of Jesus. New Testament scholars tell us that much of Mark's Gospel is based on Peter's preaching and writings. If no one of Jesus' disciples except Peter hung around the High Priest's courtyard that night, none witnessed his denial. So, he must have told on himself. He would have! Bold, transparent, Peter keeps nothing in; he tells on himself. No mystery about his character. We praise him here for the courage to confess to the appropriate ears his sin. Doesn't every reader of this episode feel the thrust of Peter's behavior straight to his own heart, "There but for the grace of God, go I"?

Peter's gnawing distress arising from a sense of guilt for his sin and his subsequent tears return us to the bird imagery. Peter, a phoenix, rises from the ashes of his own remorse. If yet alive, he could have sung the alto aria in Bach's *The Passion According to St. Matthew*:

> *Erbarme dich, mein Gott,*
> Have mercy, my God,
> *um meiner Zahren willen:*
> on my bitter tears;
> *schaue heir, Herz und Augue*
> look upon me: heart and eyes
> *weint vor dir bitterlich.*
> weep before you bitterly.
> *Erbarme dich!*
> Have mercy!

With Peter, we all say: "Jesus, have mercy upon me, a sinner."
Kyrie eleison!

A Noose
Judas Hangs Himself

When Judas saw that Jesus was condemned, he was seized with re-morse, he returned to the chief priests. "I have sinned," he cried. "I have betrayed innocent blood." They replied, "What is that to us? That's your responsibility." So Judas threw the money into the temple and left. Then he went away and hanged himself. —Matthew 27:1-5

AT THIS POINT IN MY MUSINGS ON MARK, fascination with Judas' despair necessitates turning to another gospel. Only Matthew writes up the end of Judas.

Did Mark not want to give the scoundrel any last lines on his stage which might risk the slightest rise of sympathy in his readers? Knew our fascination with the complex character of the villains of history—real and fictive: the Neros, Hitlers, Stalins, Pol Pots, Bronte's Heathcliff, Melville's Ahab, Nietzsche's Superman, Conrad's Mr. Kurtz—that Byronic hero who is passionate, moody, remorse-torn but in the end an unrepentant sinner. A fellow who is proud that he chooses to stand outside the divine moral code of good and evil.

Our fascination with Judas' motives for betrayal might distract for some moments our attention from the most important tragic hero of the night's drama. Similarly, Lucifer's muscular grandeur and eloquent phrase in Milton's *Paradise Lost* almost upstages God in that cosmic theater; one wonders about the Evil

One, "What immortal hand or eye dare frame thy fearful symmetry?" as does the narrator beholding Blake's "Tyger, Tyger, burning bright in the forests of the night."

Perhaps Mark did not want to allow any wondering about Judas which would precipitate a query such as Kahlil Gibran, the Lebanese poet, makes in his musings in *Sand and Foam*. "Was the love of Judas' mother for her son less than the love of Mary for Jesus?" Just as Mark had scrupulously not allowed any sweet birth-of-baby-Jesus narratives to intrude on the clear focus of his gospel, here, too, he keeps his eye on the mission of the suffering Christ.

Still we cannot escape wondering what motivated Judas to betray Jesus. Psychologists, cultural historians, theologians have offered their best thinking. It all boils down to one of only a few reasons:

Judas was a money lover. An avaricious adult, the child of poverty. He knew the cost of everything but nothing of its worth. Saw the washing of dirty feet with de Chanel 5 perfume, not as an anointing but an extravagance. But not a hard-bargain-driving entrepreneur—closed a deal to turn over a man on the nation's "Most Wanted" list for 30 shekels. Whether that translates to $14 or $25—or $250, by today's exchange rates—can you imagine turning in Bin Laden to the CIA for less than one million? Judas' love of money is indeed the root of his evil.

Judas was disillusioned. Perhaps he was a member of the Zealots, with their dreams of wrenching national power from the Romans. Perhaps nightly he imagined the freedom of getting the Roman boot off his Jewish neck. At first he was caught up in the excitement of Jesus' mission. Reading between the lines of Jesus' manifesto, he imagined the words "My time has not yet come" to be code for "Await the hour of revolt!" Second thoughts led to disappointment. Disappointment to disillusionment. Disillusionment to hatred. Jesus was not the Messiah Judas awaited. Let the devil take him! Judas would get on with waiting for another.

Judas miscalculated his ploy. Judas accepted Jesus as that Anointed Leader prophesied to come. But Jesus was moving too slowly. He needed a push. A week of high rehetoric in the temple courts was no longer sufficient. That weekend of the Passover and the Feast of Unleavened Bread with the city full of tens of thousands of religious pilgrims would be the time to force his Rabbi's gentle hand. But Judas saw that with the twelve keeping the festival alone in an upstairs inn, his dream could not be fulfilled. Judas would force Jesus' hand

Judas was not the first Jew to help play God. One has only to remember old Uncle Abe. Getting nervous about the promised child not bulging his wife's abdomen, at his spouse's suggestion he turned to Hagar, Sarah's Egyptian maidservant, and there helped God. But he seeded a son God called "Ishmael"—a wild ass of a man. Even today, at century's close, one reads of religious crackpots off to Israel to precipitate a crisis, if need be with a defiant act of creative insubordination—even violence—to force Jesus to return.

"I have sinned!" Judas cried to the priests, to which they sneered: "What's that to us? Look to yourself, man!" Judas then "flings the money into the temple." Meaning he stood pleading through the locked Gates Beautiful to the shepherds of his soul sequestered in the Court of the Priests. The prodigal son in Jesus' parable also cried, "I have sinned." But he found a caring father with open arms.

One thinks of Rembrandt's "Return of the Prodigal Son," hanging in the Hermitage, St. Petersburg, Russia; and of Henri Nouwen's meditations on that painting. He writes that "Judas betrayed Jesus. Peter denied him. Both were lost children. Judas, no longer able to hold on to the truth that he remained God's child, hung himself. Peter, amid his despair, claimed his sonship and returned with many tears. Judas chose death. Peter chose life. This choice is always before me. Constantly I am tempted to wallow in my own lostness and lose touch with my God-given humanity" (50). Because of that despair, Judas could not join Peter in saying, "Jesus, have mercy upon me a sinner."

Kyrie eleison!

Which Jesus?
Jesus Before Pilate

Early in the morning the chief priests handed Jesus over to Pilate.
Questioned, Jesus made no reply. His silence amazed Pilate. It was the
custom at the Feast to release a prisoner. The crowd, stirred up by the
chief priests, asked for Barabbas, the insurrectionist. "What shall I do
with the king of the Jews?" Pilate asked. "Crucify him!" they shouted.
Pilate released Barabbas and turned Jesus over to the soldiers who
mocked and flogged him. Then they led him out to crucify him.
—Mark 15: 1-20

WHICH JESUS? THE SANHEDRIN, THE religious high court, had just
found Jesus guilty of blasphemy and agreed on the death sentence (14:63-65)—an ecclesiastical, religious, moral, or spiritual
offense. An hour later, the same accusers, now before Pilate make
a different charge: this Jesus was guilty of fomenting a national-
ist uprising by calling himself the Messiah, the King of the
Jews—a political offense. So which Jesus did the religious leaders
want killed?

The chief priests knew well their oppressors, knew how to
manipulate them for their own interests, knew which buttons to
push to get a response from the Romans. The Romans would
dismiss as a silly religious argument the charge of blasphemy. But
a political charge, one of an attempted coup against imperial
Rome in Palestine—that would get Pilate's attention. Further, by

getting Rome to kill Jesus, if the populace revolted out of sympathy for their dead Rabbi, the chief priests could blame Pilate.

Which Jesus? The religious leaders made of Jesus a man to suit their needs. They wanted him removed—called him a blasphemer when the occasion suited, named him an insurrectionist when the occasion suited. But even wily Pilate knew the real reason they wanted him removed: "It was out of envy that the chief priests had handed Jesus over to him" (v. 10).

Which Jesus? Still quibbling at the cross, we Christians two thousand years later can't agree on which Jesus hung there. Those who make of Jesus' ministry a purely spiritual warfare blame the Jews, the Romans, the Zealots. These enemies misunderstood Jesus; he never meant to establish a political order but used "king" and "my kingdom" as poetic symbols common to his day. The politicians for Jesus argue that the Jewish and Roman authorities defended themselves against the possibility of a real insurrection by the common people led by Jesus. John Howard Yoder (*The Politics of Jesus*) declares that the authorities resorting to illegal procedures to rid themselves of Jesus "is a proof of the political relevance of nonviolent tactics, not a proof that Pilate and Caiaphas were exceptionally dull or dishonorable men."

Which Jesus? "Jesus," says Yoder, "was not just a moralist whose teachings had some political implications; he was not primarily a teacher of spirituality whose public ministry unfortunately was seen in a political light; he was not just a sacrificial lamb preparing for his immolation or a God-Man whose divine status calls us to disregard his humanity. Jesus was, in his divinely mandated prophethood, priesthood, and kingship, the bearer of a new possibility of human, social, and therefore political relationships" (62).

Several ironies in the events of Jesus before Pilate and the Jewish accusers give a touch of humor to these cruel hours. I hesitate mentioning "irony." Some find irony difficult to define and to illustrate. And I have no interest here in writing a treatise on figurative aspects of paradox, overstatement, understatement, and irony in literature. Suffice it to note this: Verbal irony—akin to sarcasm, satire and ridicule—is handsomely illustrated by Job with his three commiserating friends. Having listened patiently to their philosophizing about good and evil, he replied, "Doubtless you are the people, and wisdom will die with you" (12:2)! Also dramatic irony—the discrepancy between what the speaker says and what the author means. And irony of situation—that discrepancy between what one anticipates in an actual circumstance and what actually occurs. Plus other refinements of irony.

But here, broadly, the irony is of the situation. Jesus, a spiritual king of his Jewish people who refused to allow himself to lead a political uprising of their making, is then charged before the Roman political powers as being a political insurgent. Jesus' people achieve a successful accusation against Jesus for the very thing he had failed to do!

A further irony lies in the release of Barabbas—a robber (John 18:40), a murderer (Luke 23:10), an insurrectionist (Mark 15:7), a notable prisoner (Matt. 27:16). Barabbas, an actual insurgent who rallied men to rebellion, is released in place of Jesus, who refused to lead rabble.

Which Jesus? Jesus bar Abbas or Jesus bar Joseph? "Bar" being "son"—and "Abbas" meaning "father." Moffatt translates and the Revised Standard Version footnotes the full name of Barabbas as "Jesus bar-Abbas." So Pilate could rightly play with the names. "Which Jesus do you want me to release to you?" And Jesus who was flogged and crucified was the true bearer of the name: "Jesus bar-Abbas"—Jesus-the-son-of-the-Father"!

While the ironies tease the brain into a smile, the coarse mockery by the Roman guards and their horrendous flogging, the actual shredding of the back to ribbons of flesh, sting us with grief. We remember: "He was pierced for our transgressions—by his wounds we are healed" (Isa. 53:5-6). Another irony!

Niger
The Crucifixion

*Simon from Cyrene, passing by on his way in from the country, was
forced to carry Jesus' cross. They brought him to Golgotha and offered
him a mixed wine which he refused. And they crucified him on the
third hour. The charge read: "The King of the Jews." They crucified
two robbers with him. Those passing by hurled insults, as did the chief
priests and the soldiers. —Mark 15:21-32*

AGAIN WE NOTE MARK'S STYLE AS A writer: objective, restrained, elegant. These ten verses report a tragic event with the objective
voice we've come to expect in Western news writing—spare of
adjective, free of editorial comment and conjecture. The tone is
one of holding back, of reining in the emotions. A stark elegance
is the result. In his *Three Gospels*, Reynolds Price employs a luminous style so lucid as to be almost transparent; one sees the simple vertebrae of the sentence's construct of subject, verb,
complement. In Mark and Price, Jesus' crucifixion is made to
share a sentence with an ordinary activity. "Then they crucified
him and divided his clothes."

A man "passing by on his way in from the country" was
pressed into service and into the narrative line. Simon. Care was
taken to identify him by his sons, Alexander and Rufus, who
were to become prominent Roman Christians. Care was also
taken to identify him as from Cyrene, a principal city of modern

Libya, then the North African part of the Roman Empire. Writing up the Acts of the apostles in Antioch, Luke took care to identify Simon as the man "called Niger" (13:1). With that tag, Simon's African root is established.

But another person in that church at Antioch which commissioned Barnabas and Saul to an early mission venture was Lucius, also identified as being "of Cyrene," of the dark skin of Mediterranean peoples. But Simon is further distinguished from Cyrenians as a man "called Niger." *Niger*—the Latin word for "black," the root for "Negro" and its offensive corruption into "nigger." In sub-Saharan Africa, black Africa, lie the countries Niger and Nigeria, separated by French and British colonial histories, linked by the Niger River.

Thus Simon must have been a black man from Niger, from deep in West Africa, sold by Arabs in a Roman slave market in North Africa. One other reference in Acts mentions these Cyrenian Jews. In Jerusalem they had a congregation known as "the Synagogue of the Freedmen (as it was called)—Jews of Cyrene and Alexandria. . ." (6:9). "Freedmen" was a term used not only in the Roman Empire but also in America for men freed from slavery. How many Southern towns after the Civil War had a ghetto called "Freetown"!

In Jerusalem for the Jewish Passover festivities, this black African was pressed into service by the Romans. He carried Jesus' cross to Calvary, Golgotha, the Place of the Skull. A dubious honor—carried a load too heavy for Jesus, carried the instrument of his Lord's death. I say "his Lord" because something must have happened to Simon called Niger at Calvary for his name, as noted above, to pitch up later in the record of the early Christian church at Antioch, his sons with the Christian church in Rome. Then, as too often in modern history, the man Niger is pressed shamefully by the white man to do his dirty work. Later, I like to think, Simon of Niger, freed again, understood the honor of his task.

But that day, from that first meeting with this quiet bloody criminal, Simon of Niger was attracted to Jesus. He joined the other disciples to sing lamentations, some borrowed from that ancient book of poetry by the prophet Jeremiah.

Call them dirges, elegies, threnodies, lamentations, they are the poetic utterances of a people in grief. Wailings for the destruction of Jerusalem become wailings for the death of Jesus—words for our own grief at Jesus' cross. We kneel down in the face of death and desolation, as men and women everywhere have always done. Ourselves speechless with grief we listen to the poetry and music of these lamentations. For this reason God sends to us poets and singers and painters, to aid us who sit in mute shock, to give grief an articulation.

These lamentations are not the wild expressions of a grief-crazed and irrational speaker. They are the product of reflection, of "powerful emotions recollected in tranquility." No one could sit amid despair and compose an elegiac poem, write a song of sorrow. That happens later; pain in memory is transmuted into a poetry full of pathos. So we turn to art, to words from Holy Scripture, to music, to give our own grief voice.

One stands smitten before Salvador Dali's cross-nailed Christs elevated above the world; breathless in awe before Michelangelo's *Pieta* in the Vatican, of a pity melded to marble fabric and muscle so fluid they seem real. One lies listening in the dark to Henryk Gorecki's *Symphony No. 3*, translated by this symphony of sorrowful songs, one the lament of a mother for a dead son; and to his *Miserere*, to the cumulative tension of sustained subtleties of thirty minutes by an unaccompanied chorus singing "Domine Deu Noster" (Lord our God), to arrive at a resolution of a mere three minutes to sing "Miserere nobis" (have mercy upon us).

A little consoled, we "go to Jesus who suffered outside the city gate to make the people holy through his own blood. We go to him, bearing the disgrace he bore." And the music, a wide dark river of awful sound, moves through our hearts and gives voice to our lips, now, and at every memory of Jesus' crucifixion.

Why?
The Death of Jesus

At the sixth hour darkness came over the whole land until the ninth hour. Jesus cried out in a loud voice, "My God, my God, why have you forsaken me?" One man filled a sponge with wine vinegar, put it on a stick and offered it to Jesus to drink. With a loud cry, Jesus breathed his last. The curtain of the temple was torn in two from top to bottom. Some women watched from a distance. —Mark 15: 33-41

"MY GOD, MY GOD, WHY HAVE you forsaken me?" The opening line of a Psalm (22) of David now sung by this last Son of David. The second line, an antiphonic restatement: "Why are you so far from saving me, so far from the words of my groaning?" Those first nine words are a verbal eye-blink glimpse into the appalling sense of utter despair which Jesus endured. These words—"My God, why?"—that trembling cup of suffering the previous night he prayed be taken from him, is here borne to his dying lips with the strength of his own will to obey.

I think of another man who "although he [too] was a son, he learned obedience from what he suffered." Gerard Manley Hopkins, spiked to his soul-numbing duties as teacher of elementary Greek in the Jesuit university at Dublin, forged these lines, quoted here from one of his six "sonnets of desolation":

No worst, there is none. Pitched past pitch of grief,
More pangs will, schooled at forepangs, wilder wring,

Comforter, where, where is your comforting?
Mary, mother of us, where is your relief?
My cries heave, herds-long huddle in a main, a chief
Woe, world-sorrow; on an age-old anvil wince and sing—

As tradition has it, shepherd boy David declared that "The Lord is my shepherd." Did this last son of David not know that even though he walked through the valley of the shadow of death, he need fear no evil, for God was with him? Why did he cry out, "My God, my God, why have you forsaken me?" Shepherd of the Lamb—where, where is your shepherding?

Just such fears settled on me one Advent Sunday as I listened to a sermon on how the first Advent foreshadows the second Advent. That afternoon I began working at a poem which I was to refine for several more Advents. Against the terror of a possible death of a youthful son, I wrestled with God, demanding with arrogance equal rights. I felt invited to dance a rough rumba, whose step-close-step were patterned like this:

You who begot one son,
love me,
love my one begotten son.
When, before yours died, cried
"My God, my God, why—?" why
did he not cry: "Abba! Abba!"?
—"Father! Father!"—as your son?
A son should, would.
Could not? Knew your righteous-rigid
back, face turned away,
eyes widened over some faltering
sparrow not worth a farthing?
Knew you then the Yahweh, not kin?
Among us he acclaimed your character,
to emulate thus: "Be perfect, even as
my Father—" even while knowing
his hour to come, your power to go?
How could you, while you rested,

betray your spirit's flesh, his
affection, his incarnation venture?

Is this what it means to be God?
I thank you that I am man!
I will be man! I cannot be good,
will not be cruel, will not forsake a son.
Powerless before his kiss; ennobled,
His soiled hand in mine.
Yet, if perchance I fail the boy,
I—who am only your man (Your son,
made like unto one of us, faithful
to our sin-soured-selves, advocates
frailty before your perfection,
hear him, for me.)—I command,
boldly state, Sir, give me this
resurrection power too, to
restore me to him.
That which you granted yourself—
A son restored, grant me, too; you
who so loved the world, love me,
love my one begotten son.
I'll bare muscle to wrestle you for that,
though you smite me, till weakened,
I, broken, at last utter:
"So be it!"

Pieta
The Burial of Jesus

*It was the even of the Sabbath. Joseph of Arimathea, a prominent
member of the Sanhedrin, who was himself waiting for the kingdom of
God, went boldly to Pilate and asked for Jesus' body. He gave the body
to Joseph who wrapped it in a clean linen cloth and placed it in his
own new tomb that had been cut out of a rock. He rolled a big stone in
front of the entrance to the tomb. Some of the women, and Mary, sat
watching. —Mark 15:42-47*

IN HIS GOSPEL, JOHN WRITES THAT Joseph of Arimathea "was accompanied by Nicodemus, the man who earlier visited Jesus at
night. Nicodemus brought a mixture of myrrh and aloes, about
seventy-five pounds. Taking Jesus' body, the two of them
wrapped it, with spices, in strips of linen" (19:39). I much prefer
two men attending to the body of Jesus in a garden that night
outside the walled city.

Members of the supreme court of the Jews, the Sanhedrin,
that body of ecclesiastical aristocrats, they had minds as properly
conservative as the cut of their three-piece, pinstriped silk suits.
Earlier Nick, a scholarly, urbane lawyer, on a timid visit to Jesus,
asked honest, even sympathetic questions. "Rabbi, how is it possible? We know that you are a professor sent by God—how can
these things be?" And later Nick had raised a cautious legal defense of Jesus before the awesome Sanhedrin.

Now here he joined Joe, his colleague, with a supply of perfumed spices for the entombment of this Rabbi. They washed and anointed the bloodied body of a criminal, a Galilean carpenter-cum-rabbi. It was another "Pieta," more true than Michelangelo's Mary holding the body of her dying son. Perhaps even a greater "pieta"—this living statue a monument to compassion: two men, friends, holding the body of their dead friend.

Musing over this scene, I thought again of Tolstoy's *The Death of Ivan Ilych*. An increasing pain from a blow to his kidney eventually drives Ivan to bed. Although attended by celebrated doctors, he weakens until he perceives that he is dying. His illness destroys the tranquility of this bourgeois home. He learns quickly the limitations of sympathy, even from his wife and daughter. At age forty-five, "Ivan Ilych saw that he was dying, and he was in continual despair." Only his youthful son and Gerasim, a male servant, give Ivan the piteous attention he needs.

It falls to Gerasim, "a clean, fresh pleasant lad, grown stout on town food and always cheerful and bright," to toilet Ivan, a torment to him that another person had to take part in the uncleanliness, the smell. Additionally, as the pain worsened, Gerasim sat for hours, holding his master's legs on his shoulders, "willingly, simply, and with a good nature that touched Ivan Ilych." He found "in Gerasim's attitude something akin to what he wished for, and so that comforted him." Just so the affectionate male servant attended his master until dying, he utters to himself, "Death is finished."

"Be near me when I'm dying, Lord. Be near me when the light is low." The burial of Jesus by friends, the story of Gerasim and Ivan Ilych, got me to wondering this again: Who will handle my dying body? I think of this, too, when I visit the invalids at the retirement homes.

Once I said aloud to a young man, a former college student who grew to be a close friend, something of my dread should I live on with advanced Alzheimer's. Knowing the pain my situation would give to wife, children, friends, I would wish they did not visit me. At the least, I would instruct my family not to allow any of those young good friends which grew out of my years in the university classroom to visit me. Not only will I be like Ivan Ilych, in torment that another should see me. I would not want my decimated body and mind to inflict them with pain.

With a rueful smile, as if already plotting, Jason said, "You'll be out of it, too feeble to fight us; we'll take matters into our own hands. I'll be there to hold you."

Years ago Ned buried this request in a three-page letter: "Will you let me be with you when you are dying?" At first I was nearly offended, to speak to me, a man in good health, of my dying. But I read on: "You may think that question absurd, but I have been learning lately: the highest art is the one lived, not written. Sure, I send you stories which attempt to celebrate and agonize over my friendship with you, but in the end, when you are leaving this world, is my heart big enough to bear that grief? Or will I run away—to a vacation or to the demands of work? I am afraid of losing you, you who have brought me into myself."

And last year, two old student friends mailed me copies of Mitch Albom's *Tuesdays with Morrie*, inscribed with thanks and blessings. I had already read the book, my own bought copy. But I reread each gift, with months between, with the eyes of the former student, to gather some clue as to what he read in the relationship between a dying professor and a student from nearly twenty years ago.

Often chided by colleagues and family for needing to be in control of situations that involve me, I shall live up to their notions with one last request from my cedar box casket. For my penultimate will (my last, somewhere in a lawyer's box) I shall write the memorial service, prepare last words for family and friends, and name an older former student friend one last reading assignment. I hope those last words will perfume their lives, as did the friends of Jesus, even as the lives of family and friends have wrapped me with love.

Lilies and Spices
The Resurrection

When the Sabbath was over, Mary Magdalene, Mary the mother of James, and Salome bought spices so that they might go to anoint Jesus' body. Just after sunrise they made their way to the tomb. They discovered the large stone had been rolled away. As they entered the tomb, a young man dressed in a white robe said, "You're looking for Jesus. He has risen! Go tell the disciples and Peter to meet him in Galilee." Frightened, the women fled. . . and said nothing to any one.
—Mark 16:1-8

WHO KILLED JESUS? LANE AND LANE of my *Harper's Bible Dictionary* name the culprits in this brief summary: "Not the Jewish people as a whole, nor the Roman Empire alone, but a group of bigoted Jewish religious leaders and an unscrupulous foreign administrator seeking favor with the population bear the responsibility for history's greatest tragedy." I give credit to whom credit is due here to declare that the powers who killed Jesus were powerless to keep him killed.

Men betrayed, arrested, tried, convicted, crucified, and buried Jesus. But women, watching the execution from a distance, saw where Joseph and Nicodemus buried the body. After the Sabbath, the day of silence, these women move from watching in the wings to stage center. Just after sunrise they made their way to the tomb. Mark notes with one verb—"bought" (not *brought*)—the women's planning for this visit: They "bought spices so that they might go to anoint Jesus' body" (16:1). The verb "bought" raises a series of questions one cannot answer: Where did the women get money? I think these Palestinian Jewish women kept a flock of chickens and one cow (no urban planners drawing up regulations against housing livestock in Jerusalem!), as did the early American farm women.

Since they hunted eggs and churned butter and sold what their families did not consume, it was their prerogative to keep such small money to spend at their own discretion. Just so, the several Marys and Salome shook out together from their hidden sources the coins needed to barter for spices and aloes. They would have to barter hard—prices jacked up because of all the tourists in town for the Passover.

When did the women make the purchase? Shops, closed on the Sabbath, had hardly opened before sunrise on the day after the Sabbath. So they bought the needed spices in the early evening of Jesus' crucifixion, minutes before the shops closed for the Sabbath, which began at sundown. So Good Friday was indeed the Day of Preparation, as the day before the Sabbath was called by the Jews! They'd seen Nicodemus' servants tote in seventy-five pounds of myrrh and aloes, spices sufficient for one burial. Still the women wanted to join in "The Festival of the Lord's Death."

Of course, busy old gospeler Luke takes all the fun out of conjecture, of writing an imaginary script for these grieving women who wanted to make their own private tribute. Luke writes that "The women who had come with Jesus from Galilee followed Joseph and saw the tomb and how his body was laid in it. Then they went home and prepared spices and perfumes. But they rested on the Sabbath in obedience to the commandment" (22:55-56).

I'll take it from there! Begrudgingly, I'll admit I like Luke's account better than Mark's. The gift made in one's kitchen is always better than the one bought in a shop. The loaves of home-baked, whole wheat and honey bread forced on one's children as Christmas gifts for their elementary teachers were received with genuine thanks; a slice of such a gift was more intoxicating than any perfume from the mall.

My first university reading of Faulkner was under an old Southern gentleman. Doc Adams explained that the flowers which Miss Jenny Sartoris Dupre (in the novels *Sartoris* and *Sanctuary*, and the stories "There Was a Queen" and "An Odor of Verbena") cut from her own gardens, even if they yielded a slightly wispy bouquet, were of greater social weight than any $25 arrangement from a florist shop. Gifts from one's kitchen and garden carried the warmth of the giver. Bought gifts were vulgar, redolent of a mere mercantile transaction.

I suspect that giving flowers at illness and at death has been around for centuries. As was the giving of spices and perfumes at the time of Jesus. I do not know such histories, nor whether flowers have supplanted spices in today's Mediterranean countries. But I can imagine that both gifts had at first a practical side. Those centuries before embalming became a custom, one welcomed something to mask the odor of death in the house. Bring in the perfume of spices and aloes, bring in the cloy of hyacinth and lily!

Easter comes too early in my mid-Atlantic state to cut flowers from my garden as a Rejoice Offering for my church on Easter morning. So when I took a year's turn as the person responsible for weekly floral arrangements, and having a budget greater and more easily accessible than my imagination—I, too, went off to the flower merchants and bought the ubiquitous white Easter lilies. Actually I bought so many I had them delivered by the florist in her van! Were I responsible to flank the pulpit this Easter with lilies, I'd stand among the flowers tall glass decanters of perfumed spices and fragrant potpourri. Even the literal meaning of that word *potpourri*—"rotten pot"—would remind me, not only of a mixture of dried flowers, herbs, and spices, but also of the decaying flesh which the resurrected Christ lay aside to rise in a differently constituted body.

"The Lord is Risen!"

"He is risen indeed!"

Denouement
The Commission
and the Ascension

When Jesus rose early on the first day of the week, he appeared first to Mary Magdalene. They told those who had been with him weeping. Afterwards Jesus appeared in a different form to two walking in the country. Later Jesus appeared to the Eleven as they were eating; he rebuked them for their lack of faith. Then he said, "Go into all the world and preach the good news. Those who believe will drive out demons, speak in new tongues, pick up snakes, drink deadly poison—it will not hurt them at all." After that the Lord Jesus was taken up into heaven and he sat at the right hand of God. The disciples went out and preached everywhere. —Mark 16:9-20

Yes! Yes! Yes! I know what eminent New Testament scholars say about this last passage of Mark: The most reliable early manuscripts and other ancient witnesses do not have Mark 16:9-20. The last pages of the hand-penned original manuscript being passed from hand-to-hand (but not too many hands, of course, with literacy low even among Palestinian Jews)—somehow got torn off. So some committee took on writing a summary of those pages, as best they could remember. (Another "potpourri" I want to say—better, a pastiche or hodgepodge—just the kind of thing you get from cooperative authorship, or worse, an editor who wrote nothing more in his life than letters of rejection to writers!)

But that seems as probable an explanation as any—last pages getting torn off. Some paperback books in my own little library show that wear, books loaned to one's children (and now to a granddaughter reading at three!) or to the poor but literate students, and those too tight to buy their own books, saving their money to purchase another CD by Madonna—the ertwhile mocker of virginity, not the Virgin.

I care not a blasted fig for the last words of Mark's Gospel but am pleased someone—whether Jew or Greek, hardly French, also wanted a denouement to this book-length narrative. This classic needed a classic ending. The times were hardly modern, certainly not postmodern, with a style truncated and open-ended. Mark's gospel was handsomely written, long before our century's modern theories of literature and criticism.

And one couldn't just let the story end with "Trembling and bewildered, the women went out and fled from the tomb. They said nothing to anyone, because they were afraid." Frightened bewildered? Yes, probably. But frightened and bewildered women "saying nothing"? Not likely: I have it on the best of authority, polling one wife, two daughters, two granddaughters!

So let us have a *denouement*—that Frenchy term applicable to either comedy or tragedy for plotting the end of a literary piece. The term means "unknotting." So the action, intrigue, success, failure, mystery, or misunderstanding for the protagonist—here Jesus—is all cleared away. And this with no "Deus ex Machina"—Latin for "a god from a machine," to describe the practice of Greek playwright Euripides to end a drama with a god lowered to the stage by a mechanical apparatus to judge, command, solve, or wipe up a human mess. Anyway, here with Jesus' ascension, it is the reverse of a god descending!

I came home from my first three-year missionary sojourn in Somalia to find that a missionary statesman I admired, who inspired me, even at my commission service in Weaverland Church, had published a book. My mission-fired mind then stoked afresh. Yet nothing J. D. Graber wrote in his published Conrad Grebel Lecture, *The Church Apostolic*—fine writing that it is—quite appealed to me as the poem he selected for the preface. Was the poet in me, even as a furloughed missionary, daring to push up its tight sleepy bud for nourishment? Whatever, here's the poem, entitled "Missionaries," by a Henry Barnett:

> Who are these that run along the highways of the world
> And seek its meanest suburbs with their feet?
> They are the troubadours of God,
> Blowing an airy melody along earth's aisles
> As solid as the masonry of dreams.
> They are the wise eccentrics
> Who reason with divine hilarity.
> They are the canny merchants
> Who buy the hearts of nations for their Prince.
> They are vivid tailors
> Who push the thread of ages through their hands.
> They are the white militia
> Who take no blood to spill it, save their own.
> They are the blessed coolies
> Who lift the loads of folly on their backs,
> And dump them into truth's dissolving streams.
> They are the blithe outrunners
> Who trek the world's long reaches for old trails
> Whereon to lay the pavement of new years.
> They are the grave cross-bearers
> Who bear stern wooden gibbets on their backs,
> And nail their loves and treasures to the beams.
> They are our princely brothers,
> Born of the womb which bore us,
> Who speak for us amid the courts of life.

Yes! Yes! Yes! Not dour Puritans to Hawaii nor the black-frock pioneers of my own tribe to Africa—both fine in the fire of their days. But now, witnesses as "wise eccentrics," as "troubadours," as "canny merchants," "vivid tailors," "blithe outrunners"! Still they clutch the promise, "I am with you, to the end of the age"!

Sources

King James Version of the Bible

Revised Standard Version of the Bible

The Gospel of Mark. Trans. William Barclay. Philadelphia: Westminster Press, 1954.

The Holy Bible. New International Version.

The Modern Reader's Bible. Trans. Richard Moulton. New York: Macmillan, 1952.

The New English Bible (with the Apocrypa). Oxford: Oxford University Press, and Cambridge: Cambridge University Press, 1970.

The New Testament in Modern English. Trans. J. B. Phillips. New York: Macmillan, 1960.

Three Gospels. Trans. Reynolds Price. New York: Simon and Schuster, 1996.

Abrams, M. J., gen. ed., et al. *The Norton Anthology of English Literature*, 2 vols. fourth ed. New York: Norton, 1979.

Baker, Herschel, ed. *The Later Renaissance in England.* Boston: Houghton Mifflin, 1975.

Baldwin, James. *Going to Meet the Man.* New York: Dial Press, 1948.

Becker, Ernest. *The Denial of Death.* New York: Free Press, 1973.

———. *Escape From Freedom.* New York: Free Press, 1975.

Bonhoeffer, Dietrich. *The Cost of Discipleship.* New York: Macmillan, 1963.

———. *Letters and Papers from Prison.* New York: Macmillan, 1953.

———. *Life Together.* New York: Harper and Brother, 1954.

Buechner, Frederick. *The Clown in the Belfry*. San Francisco: Harper-Collins, 1992.

Ciardi, John. *A Browser's Dictionary: A Compendium of Curious Expressions and Intriguing Facts*. New York: HarperCollins, 1980.

Conrad, Joseph. *Heart of Darkness*. New York: Penguin, 1989.

Crossman, John Dominic. *Jesus: A Revolutionary Biography*. San Francisco: HarperCollins, 1995.

Dillard, Annie. *For the Time Being*. New York: Knopf, 1999.

———.*Pilgrim at Tinker Creek*. New York: Harpers, 1974.

Dostoevsky, Fyodor. *The Brothers Karamazov*. New York: New American Library, 1957.

Faulkner, William. *Intruder in the Dust*. New York: Modern Library, 1948.

Frankl, Viktor. *Man's Search for Meaning*. Boston: Beacon Press, 1959.

Gardner, Helen, ed. *The Metaphysical Poets*. New York: Penguin, 1981.

Gasztold, Carmen Bernos de. *The Creatures Choir*. New York: Viking, 1965.

———. *Prayers from the Ark*. New York: Viking, 1962.

Gibran, Kahlil. *Sand and Foam*. London: Heinemann, 1954.

Graber, J.D. *The Church Apostolic*. Scottdale: Herald Press, 1960.

Greene, Graham. *The Power and the Glory*. New York: Penguin, 1977.

Hammarskjold, Dag. *Markings*. New York: Knopf, 1966.

Hawthorne, Nathaniel. *The Scarlet Letter*. Boston: Houghton, Mifflin, 1960.

Hemingway, Ernest. *Farewell to Arms*. New York: Scribner, 1961.

Hopkins, Gerard Manley. *Poems*. London: Studio Vista, 1960.

Jones, Alan. *Exploring Spiritual Direction*. New York: Harper and Row, 1982.

Joyce, James. *A Portrait of the Artist as a Young Man*. New York: Penguin, 1977.

Kierkegaard, Soren. *Works of Love*. New York: Harpers, 1962.

Lane, Belden. *The Solace of Fierce Landscapes*. New York: Oxford University Press, 1998.

Lewis, C. S. *The Four Loves*. New York: Harcourt, Brace and World, 1960.

———. *Letters to Malcolm: Chiefly on Prayer*. New York: Harcourt, Brace and World, 1963.

———. *Mere Christianity*. New York: Macmillan, 1958.

———. *The Problem of Pain*. New York: Macmillan, 1963.

———. *Surprised by Joy*. New York: Harcourt, Brace and World, 1955.

———. *The World's Last Night and Other Essays*. New York: Harcourt, Brace and Co., 1960.

Melville, Herman. *Billy Budd*. New York: Harper and Row, 1970.

Merton, Thomas. *New Seeds of Contemplation*. New York: New Directions, 1961.

———. *The Wisdom of the Desert*. New York: New Directions, 1970.

———. *Spiritual Direction and Meditation*. Collegeville: Liturgical Press, 1960.

Miller, Madeleine, and J. Lane Miller. *Harper's Bible Dictionary*. New York: Harper and Row, 1973.

Milton, John. *Complete Poems*. New York: Odyssey, 1957.

Nietzsche, Friedrich. *Beyond Good and Evil*. New York:Random, 1966.

Nouwen, Henri. *The Wounded Healer*. New York: Doubleday. 1972.

———. *The Genesee Diary*. New York: Doubleday, 1976.

———. *Life of the Beloved*. New York: Crossroad, 1993.

———. *The Return of the Prodigal Son*. New York: Doubleday, 1972.

Paton, Alan. *The Long View*. New York: Praeger, 1968.

Peck, M. Scott. *People of the Lie*. New York: Simon and Schuster, 1983.

Price, Reynolds. *Letter to a Man in the Fire*. New York: Scribner. 1999.

Robinson, Barbara. *The Best Christmas Pageant Ever*. New York: Harper and Row, 1972.

Swartley, Willard M. *Mark: The Way for All Nations*. Scottdale: Herald Press, 1979.

Webster, Douglas. *Yes to Mission*. London: SCM Press, 1966.

Yoder, John Howard. *The Politics of Jesus*. Grand Rapids: Eerdmans 1972.

Zylstra, Henry. *Testament of Vision*. Grand Rapids: Eerdmans, 1958.

The Author

OMAR EBY, HARRISONBURG, VIRGINIA, taught for six years in Africa, including in Mogadishu, Somalia; Musoma, Tanzania; and Kitwe, Zambia. He took graduate degrees in journalism from Syracuse University and creative writing from the University of Virginia. He holds the B.A. in English from Eastern Mennonite University, where he taught writing and literature for 27 years before taking early retirement to pursue his own writing. Eby has published books of fiction, biography, and personal experience.